I Love You Rituals

Activities to Build Bonds and Strengthen Relationships with Children

By Dr. Becky Bailey

Loving Guidance

Published by:

Loving Guidance
P. O. Box 622407
Oviedo, Florida 32762
1-800-842-2846

Publisher's Cataloging in Publication

Bailey, Rebecca Anne, 1952 -
    I love you rituals: activities to build bonds and strengthen relationships with children/by Becky Anne Bailey.
    ISBN: 1-889609-05-6

Library of Congress Catalog Card Number: 97-0594
1. Parent and child - Psychological aspects.
2. Parental influences
3. Child Rearing
4. Title

HQ769.635.1996   306.874

QB196-20405

Every effort has been made to trace the ownership of all copyrighted material and to secure the necessary permissions to reprint these selections. In the event of any questions arising as to the use of any material, the editor and publisher, while expressing regret for any inadvertent error, will be happy to make the necessary correction in future printings.

BOOK DESIGN: Bell Vision Visual Communications
COVER ILLUSTRATION: Marshall Lloyd
ILLUSTRATIONS: Jeff Jones
AUTHOR PHOTOGRAPH: Tim Twe

Contents

I love you rituals put life in focus, shifting from getting ahead to getting
together and from valuing material wealth to valuing one another.

INTRODUCTION

"Everybody longs to be loved. And the
greatest thing we can do is let somebody
know that they are loved and
capable of loving."

—— Fred Rogers

During the past ten years, I have been concerned about the growing number of children who seem not to be enjoying childhood and the growing number of adults who seem not to be enjoying adulthood. Some children just seem anxious. Others are clearly unhappy, demonstrating this with violent outbursts and aggressive tendencies. Adults seem compulsive, hurried, and worried. I know that these faces of anxiety are not real, just masks the children are wearing over their true selves. How can these masks be lifted? Where are our true children? How can the masks of adults be lifted? Where are our true adults? The answer is in finding one another. In our hurried lifestyles we have lost something. We all seem to be feeling a bit disconnected and separate. This isolation appears rooted in a need to protect ourselves from hurt, hide parts of ourselves from each other, and cover up deep feelings of inadequacy. It seems to me we are not lost causes, just simply lost.

In my own journey to reconnect with myself and others, Pat Clark, friend and colleague, and I began studying Developmental Play by Viola Brody and Theraplay by the late Ann Jernberg. I am indebted to the wisdom of these great women. These were life-changing experiences for me. Each of these approaches requires the adult to be present, in the moment, engaged with children. If you had asked me before this training, "Becky, do you believe you are truly present with children when you interact with them?" I would have responded with a definite "yes." I came to discover that this was not accurate. I, like many of you, have been socialized to think either of the past (what I should have done) or think to the future (what I need to do next). The present was an illusive commodity for me.

As I began my personal journey, I found out something very surprising: I was frightened" of the present moment. The present was where my feelings were located. I had spent so many years staying busy, exercising, achieving, taking care of others, I never realized these were different forms of compulsion to drown out my feelings. I also thought that if I relaxed and let down my defenses, people would see me as incompetent or as not worthy. What I discovered was that when I chose to relax and be in the present, I felt connected and loved. My fears melted away. The more I could stay in the moment, the more I could engage with children. Just think about it. If young children live in the present and adults spend most of their time in the past or in the future, we have abandoned our children to some degree.

This book, I Love You, Rituals, came out of my journey from being lost in the past and projecting in the future to rediscovering myself in the present. I once read, "The true gifts of life lie in the moment. That is, why we call it the present." We, as a culture, have replaced presence with presents.

Each moment we have a choice to be fully present and loving or to be disconnected and distant. *I Love You Rituals* were created in my moments with children. They have truly been gifts to me. I have had the privilege of connecting with some wonderful children. Each of these children, in their own way, demanded I stay present with them. For those children and the moments we spent together, I am thankful.

As with any endeavor, this book came about through a synergy of people and events. I originally sat at the computer to work on a book entitled "Conscious Discipline." Instead, this book is what came forth. I was blessed with inspiration and am appreciative. I want to acknowledge my godchild, Etta June Delanoy. She played many of these rituals with me and helped me more clearly define the hand positions. Kate O'Neil willingly stood in as a guinea pig if no children were available. She taught me the value of these experiences for adults as well as children. Jeff Jones, the artist, had the task not only of being creative but also of drawing some of the more intricate hand positions. Mary Gayle Guidon and Monica Klisz created the cover and designed the layout of the book. Their design creativity captured the essence of the book. Keith McIntyre read my original drafts and guided me to clarity. Dr. Penny Leggett and my mother, Frances Bailey, further edited the book. The final proofing of the book was done by my dear friend Linda Gill. She, as always, made time in her busy life to support me and my work. For all these people, I am grateful.

The mentor teachers from the University of Central Florida and Orange County Public Schools' early childhood program, led by Carolyn Brookes and Sarah Sprinkel, field tested these rituals with all kinds of children. Their response and participation was very validating and invaluable.

Dr. Robert Schuller once called me, "my new friend Becky Bailey." I am grateful to Dr. Schuller who indeed has been a true friend in supporting my work. His positive message has inspired and helped me as well as millions of other people.

Finally, I would like to thank those people in my life who taught me about rituals - my family. Thank you, Mom and Dad, for your consistent gifts of love to me. When I was younger, I used to get pains in my stomach. My Grandmother Canipe would have me lie on the couch, and she would sit down in such a way that I would curl around her. As the pains eventually disappeared, I continued to sit with her on the couch in this fashion. I watched television while she snapped beans. It became an "I love you ritual" for us. I am so grateful for those moments, and even though she passed away over twenty years ago, through our ritual her presence is still with me. These *I Love You Rituals* are my present to your presence. Good journey!

This book is dedicated to this very moment;
may we all choose to experience it.

CHAPTER 1

I Love You Rituals:
Why Adults and Children
Need These Now!

"From a little spark may
burst a mighty flame."

— Dante

I Love You Rituals are delightful interactions and games adults can play with children from infancy to eight years of age, which send the message of unconditional acceptance. Unconditional acceptance is love. These activities are designed to build bonds and strengthen relationships between adults and children. They are written for children who are happy and children who are hurting. In our fast-paced world of the nineties, time to just "be" with our children seems to be on the verge of extinction. These playful activities, conducted in just minutes, remove all longing created from time apart, allow disagreements to dissolve, and promote love and respect for one another.

All cultures across time have created rituals. Rituals are a central part of life, whether in how meals are shared together or in how major events and holidays are marked. Rituals surround us, from the common birthday ritual of making a wish before you blow out the candle to bedtime routines that may involve sayings such as "Sleep tight, don't let the bedbugs bite." Rituals create time to be playful, to explore the meaning of our lives, and to rework and rebuild relationships. Think of the pleasant rituals from your childhood. What feeling is evoked as you allow yourself to reminisce the experience? Generally, it is a feeling of love, warmth and safety. For those moments, "all is well" with yourself, your family, and the world. One woman shared her ritual of "sniffing" her granddaughter when they hugged each other. As silly as this may sound, the meaning for both grandmother and granddaughter will last a lifetime.

"I Love You Rituals are delightful interactions and games adults can play with children from infancy to eight years of age that send the message of unconditional acceptance."

14

With the changing face of society, we are awestruck by how different families are today than they were twenty or fifty years ago. The same is true in educational settings. The challenges faced by teachers in the nineties do not compare to those addressed decades ago. As our society restructures itself with shifting gender roles, blended families, cultural diversity, and economic and political uncertainty, fear is a prevalent emotion. New rituals are needed for families, for teachers, and for children. *I Love You Rituals* put life in focus, shifting from getting ahead to getting together and from valuing material wealth to valuing one another. They are called rituals because they are designed to be part of the day-to-day activities between adults and children. Parents may decide an I Love You Ritual is a perfect interaction to facilitate reconnecting with their child when picking him up from school. Teachers may find certain games make excellent rituals for greeting children in the morning. Pick a time, pick a place, and consistently engage your child in these activities every day. The ritual has then begun.

When I am conducting workshops, I always encourage adults to touch their children as well as each other. If the workshop is filled with educators, I often hear, "We are told not to touch the children," because schools fear possible lawsuits. These teachers are working with children anywhere from three years old and up. I am bewildered at how a society as advanced as ours has lost sight of something as basic as caring touch. When I ask adults in these workshops to conduct activities together, I am repeatedly told of their discomfort in touching one another. It is common to hear, "I could do this easily with children. I just find the game difficult with another adult." These comments are usually from women. Many men just refuse to engage in the activities. We have created many rationalizations why we are not to touch one another. We have become a society of untouchables. It is becoming much easier to shop and buy presents for one another than to hug one another. Young infants are placed in infant seats to be carried, in car seats for sporting, and in bassinets or cribs to sleep. We are becoming trained to touch babies only when they demand our attention. With time the commodity most sought by modern parents, a quiet baby willing to entertain herself in the infant carrier frees parents to attend to life's other demands. Unfortunately, as we focus on other demands such as careers, our children are becoming demanding.

I Love You Rituals are based on caring touch. In 1920, Dr. Henry Chapin, a New York pediatrician, reported the death rate for infants under two years of age in institutions across the United States was 100 percent. These infants received adequate food and shelter. What was missing was caring touch for these babies. He concluded that being handled, carried, cuddled, and caressed was necessary for life. Experiments since Dr. Chapins's publication continue to support his conclusions. Research indicates that with animals and humans alike, the behavior of those receiving caring touch is strikingly different from those who don't. All animals (including humans) who received large quantities of caring touch were relaxed, cooperative, had strong immune systems, possessed an overall better functioning physiology, were friendly, and were better able to handle all forms of stress. The animals who did not receive adequate touch were timid, apprehensive, and high-strung. They were frequently tense, resistant, and often aggressive. The animals or children studied were generally described as hyper, impulsive, anxious, and irritable. With millions of our children on ritalin for hyperactivity, one cannot help but wonder about the relationship between time for caring touch and current educational and parenting practices.

Touch is much more a metaphor in our society than a reality. When we speak of someone who is removed from reality, we say that he is "out of touch." We speak of people who have a "magic touch" or a "professional touch." We speak of someone who is quick to take offense or overly sensitive as "touchy." We never really feel secure unless we can "hold onto something," nor do we really believe that we understand anything until we have a "firm grip on it." *I Love You Rituals* give us permission to move from the symbolic expression of touch to a caring touch. Somewhere, somehow, we lost "touch" with ourselves and our children. We have grown so distant from each other that permission, as well as a structure for touching one another is necessary.

I Love You Rituals are simple little games, similar to peek-a-boo and patty cake, that many of us played with our babies. They involve togetherness, touch, ritualization, and sheer joy and delight. They are designed to be played with happy children in loving classrooms and homes, as well as with hurting children who have unmet needs.

I Love You Rituals and Disciplining Children: A Powerful Connection.

Each of us wants to give unconditional love to children, yet we frequently find ourselves in the role of setting limits and conditions on children's behavior and activities. We are constantly giving commands and reminders: "Get in your car seat, put on your seat belt, finish your homework, pick up those toys, find your shoes." We find ourselves repeatedly saying no: "You may not play in the street, you can't have any candy, stop hitting your brother." Whether we are teachers or parents, we seem to spend a lot of time saying or implying, "If you do _____, then you may _____." Sometimes the fun activities children enjoy are used as rewards, and therefore, they too become conditional.

If we honestly take a look at our day, the amount of unconditional attention we give our children is minimal. Think about all the things you do with and for your children. From this mental list remove all the things that you feel you have to do (your responsibilities as a parent or teacher), all the things you do out of guilt because you think you fell short on your obligations, and all the time you spend reminding or disciplining. How much time is left for the sheer enjoyment of each other? It is time to let go of obligations and guilt and shift our perspective. *I Love You Rituals* are part of this process.

Discipline and guiding the behavior of young children is a difficult task for most adults. *I Love You Rituals* are an integral part of any discipline approach you may choose to use, whether you are dealing with children who are happy (generally have their needs met) or children who are hurting (currently have unmet needs). Take time and think about this next sentence very carefully. The motivation to behave comes from being in relationship with one another. Historically, we have believed that to motivate children to behave in ways we approve of, we have to get them to feel bad. We remove privileges, send them to time out, shout, and lecture.

Most adults want children to be cooperative members of a family or classroom. We want children to "choose" to behave well. Are you more cooperative when you feel connected to others or when you are feeling unlovable and inadequate? To discipline children we must build strong, healthy relationships with them. We have a choice: we can make time to give unconditionally to our children and develop healthy relationships, or we can be too busy or tired and create demanding children who get our attention in inappropriate ways. Our children *will* get our attention, the question is how. The answer is up to us.

TWO COMMON MISTAKES ADULTS MAKE WITH CHILDREN

1. We get caught up in our obligations and tasks and lose sight of our children until they "get in trouble" (displease us) or "do something special" (please us). During both of these occasions, the children receive our full and undivided attention. We could call one negative attention and the other positive attention. Neither is helpful or healthy. Children come to learn that in order to be "loved" (i.e., get attention) they must either misbehave or be special. These two positions require the child to be less than others (in trouble) or better than others (winning). This becomes a vicious cycle. The real reason adults get caught up in obligations is their need to avoid feeling less than others or their need to feel better than others to maintain their own sense of self-esteem. To keep their children from this same pitfall, adults must take charge and establish strong relationships with children. Adults must make time to "be" with their children. This time must be commanded and orchestrated by adults, not demanded by children. *I Love You Rituals* can be the beginning of this process whereby adults regain control of themselves and stay in charge of children.

2. Often adults find themselves locked in negative patterns of interactions with their children. As the child grows and challenges the adults around him or her more, constant battles can be the norm instead of the exception. These battles can be especially trying during the toddler years. As these battles continue day in and day out, the relationship between the adult and child

becomes strained. The willingness to begin the healing process must come from the adult, but many adults just don't know what to do. The question becomes, how do we "make up" with our children without giving in to them? How do we begin meeting the needs of children on our terms instead of theirs? What can be done? What will heal the relationship? The answer is *I Love You Rituals*. When your relationship with a child has become challenging, make time for an I Love You Ritual in the morning and in the evening. As you add these moments of unconditional love to your relationship, you will be inviting cooperation into your home or classroom.

I LOVE YOU RITUALS ARE MORE THAN FUN!

For children who are happy and children who are hurting, *I Love You Rituals* serve the following functions:

1. They create a space of fun, joy, and laughter as they build and strengthen the relationship between adult and child. As these relationships grow, young children are better able to create healthy relationships with peers and siblings.

2. They are an expression of unconditional acceptance. They are a method of delivering the message of acceptance to children. For these brief moments both adults and children get to step outside the restrictions placed on us and just experience one another.

3. They motivate children to be more cooperative. This cooperation carries over into the home as children become more willing to do chores, get along with siblings, and choose to obey their parents more often. The same increases occur in school as children become more willing to attend, complete tasks, and socialize.

4. They will increase children's attention spans. These interactions require the adult and child to attend to one another. Through this process the child learns to modulate his or her own arousal systems and begins to maintain more self-control. A child who attends and maintains self-control learns more.

5. They provide a means for reconnecting with each other after conflicts in relationships. All relationships involve disagreements. Adults make up with each other through communication. *I Love You Rituals* are a means of concretely communicating with young children in a manner they can feel. The interactions move beyond words, speak to the essence of who we are, and provide the healing needed.

6. They are ritualized so children begin to predict their occurrence and count on the reassurances they provide. They begin to know that regardless of their behavior or mistakes, they will be ultimately accepted and loved.

7. They remind us of the love that we are. Sometimes we get grumpy, negative, and oppositional. We forget that we are lovable and loved. *I Love You Rituals* are reminders of the joy of ourselves and each other. They allow us to rework and rebuild the image of ourselves and children. This helps shift the world from fear to love.

The main difference between conducting *I Love You Rituals* with children who are happy and children who are hurting is the response to the interactions the adult receives from the child. It is important to remember that *I Love You Rituals* are fun and helpful for children who are happy; however, they are essential for children who are hurting.

I Love You Rituals and Children Who Are Happy

I Love You Rituals will be helpful and fun for parents, caregivers, and teachers who want to increase joy, acceptance, trust, and honesty in their relationships with children. Children who are happy generally adore these interactions. You might hear "do it again" if you are a parent. If you are a teacher, you might hear "do me next." The children will melt into your arms, relax their bodies, giggle with delight, and totally attend to you.

I Love You Rituals and Children Who Are Hurting

I Love You Rituals are essential for teachers, caregivers, or parents of children who hurt. Children who are hurting are at risk of becoming children who hate. Children who are hurting are wonderful kids, but something sad or hurtful has happened in their lives. They are anxious and frightened - some neglected and some abused. They have lost trust in adults; perhaps they have never experienced trust. Without a trusting relationship, children lose faith in themselves, others, and the world, becoming locked in self-defeating attitudes and actions. These children have become angry, antagonistic, withdrawn, or defensive. Individually they can become a handful to deal with, and in group settings their behaviors challenge even the best educator or parent.

Children who hurt often have lost someone with whom they had a close bond. Stressful situations - divorce, death, fights, suicide - all convey the message that life in the family is unsafe. Some family relationships are seriously infected with rejection, criticisms, violence, contradictions, and neglect. Children believe that no one cares for them. They learn that adults are not to be trusted and that sometimes they make decisions or do things that hurt others. Children in stressful family situations blame themselves. Children who hurt come from all walks of life. Their inappropriate behaviors are pleas for unqualified acceptance and love as well as appropriate guidance.

The good news is young children with pain can heal! The healing will not come through words or specific disciplinary actions but will occur in the relationship you establish with them. Many of these children have never been in a healthy bonded relationship with an adult. Therefore their relationship with authority is unhealthy and will continue to be so unless an adult intervenes. Children who hurt need an adult willing to make a commitment to them. To help these children heal from their hurts, a relationship built with a caring adult based on acceptance and love is needed. If you have ever lived in an area that experienced a drought, you noticed that the grass turns brown and stops growing. When you pour water on dry ground, the earth resists the water it so desperately needs. The water bubbles up almost like oil floating on water, but if you continue to flood the area, the resistance of the earth recedes and the water is accepted. Children who hurt are in a drought condition. The first love you offer them, they may resist. As we flood them with our persistence and commitment to their beauty, their resistance ceases and the love is accepted. This book is for all the children and adults who hurt.

These activities and the concurrent result of playing them are essential in order for young children who are hurting to successfully interact in group settings such as school. You cannot expect children who have not experienced love, acceptance, compassion, gentle touches, or responsiveness to be able to interact effectively in group settings. You cannot give what you do not have. Children who are happy see other children as possible friends. Children who are hurting see other children as competition for scarce resources.

Many children who are hurting have problems forming bonds and attachments. They may resist these activities at first. Their resistance might be verbal ("This is for babies") or physical (looking away or pretending to fall asleep). Our job is to persist in having fun and staying engaged, regardless of the responses of indifference received from the child. The ultimate task is to establish and develop a relationship built on acceptance. This will enable children to change their view of themselves and ultimately their view of the world, which will lead to changes in their behavior.

A second-grade teacher shared a story that involved herself and a child in her classroom who had experienced a great deal of pain in his young life. Gary had entered public school as a kindergartner. He immediately was labeled as a child with problems. During his first two years of school, Gary was diagnosed but not helped. His behavior and academic skills continued to worsen as time went on. When he entered second grade, his teacher decided to make a commitment to establishing a relationship with him. Every morning when Gary arrived at school, his teacher would greet him warmly and touch her forehead to his and say, "I am so glad to see you and so glad you are in my class." Gary would withdraw from the touch, mumble under his breath, and shrug his shoulders as if not caring about the greeting, the touch, or the teacher. The teacher continued this I Love You Ritual for 179 days of the 180-day school year. Each day Gary did not show one sign that this ritual had meaning for him or that he cared whether it occurred or not. The teacher, committed to Gary, persisted in her desire to reach him. On the final day of school, the teacher became preoccupied with the class goodbye party and forgot to greet Gary. For the first time in Gary's school life, he sought out another person, initiated contact, and spoke. He walked over and leaned against the teacher. He stroked her hair and said, "You forgot our thing this morning." Gary and his teacher had both been touched literally and figuratively. These small moments, unconditionally given by the adult to the child, changed both their lives.

"Children who are happy see other children as possible friends. Children who are hurting see other children as competition for scarce resources."

25

CHAPTER 2

The Most Important Thing We Do:
The Bonding Process

"The main source of good
discipline is growing up in a
loving family, being loved and
learning to love in return."

—— Benjamin Spock

Young children possess varying abilities to establish and maintain close relationships with others. This ability to establish healthy relationships is related to the quality of the attachment the child has had with his or her primary caregivers during infancy, as well as other factors such as temperament and genetics.

The bonding process begins in the mother's womb, and the attachment process continues after birth. When an affectionate, healthy bond develops between children and their primary caregivers, it allows children to develop trust in themselves and others and lays the groundwork for future psychological, physical, and cognitive development. A healthy attachment or bonding process provides a secure base from which developing children can move out and explore their environment.

Attachment results, in part, in response to the arousal-relaxation cycle that occurs in the interactions between the infant and the primary caregivers. In this cycle, the infant experiences some need. For our example, let's say the infant is hungry. As the infant experiences this need, a state of arousal becomes her internal experience. If a caregiver responds to this need relatively quickly, the internal state of arousal or distress stops and the infant experiences a state of relaxation. This process, repeated over and over again, becomes associated with specific caregivers. Whatever is associated with a specific caregiver is then generalized to the rest of the world. For a securely bonded infant, the world is a safe place in which to grow. This lens from which she views the world is then carried through life, unless some significant event is experienced that alters her view of relationships.

The Arousal-Relaxation-Attachment Cycle

Problems in this cycle can occur at any point along the way. For example, a baby with colic will experience a need and a state of arousal coming from an internal stressor. Even though the caregiver responds to the baby immediately,

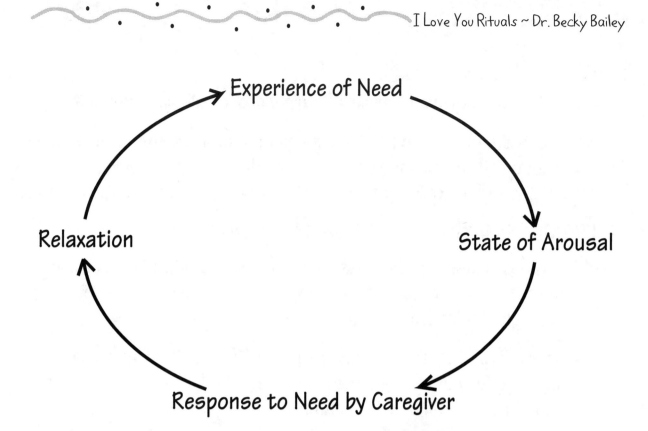

his responses do not necessarily relieve the internal pains of the baby and the relaxation part of the cycle is not obtained. Or another example is found in a crowded, infant day care center. Ashley, a six-week-old infant, signals a need to the caregivers by crying. The two caregivers already are meeting the needs of other infants, so Ashley is ignored. Ashley then misses the relaxation cycle, and concurrently associates these unpleasant feelings with the caregivers specifically and the world in general. The world is an anxious place in which she must strategize and cope. This lens from which she views the world is carried through life unless other events foster a different view of relationships. Think of a number of examples or situations that would interfere with this important bonding cycle and check your list with the list below.

Problems in the attachment process may be the result of problems concerning the infant or problems with the environment in which the infant is growing.

1. PROBLEMS MAINLY WITH THE INFANT

✔ A child may not experience pleasure or comfort because he has a higher than normal threshold for pain and discomfort, as in the case of premature infants, many of whom experience a great deal of internal discomfort.

✔ Caregivers try to respond to the baby but are unsuccessful in relieving the discomfort. This occurs frequently with children who have organic problems such as colic, birth complications or chronic ear infections.

2. PROBLEMS MAINLY WITH THE ENVIRONMENT

✔ Caregivers continually fail to respond to the child's attaching behaviors (smiling, crying, eye contact, reaching, etc.), as in the case of severe child neglect or inadequate infant day care.

✔ Caregivers consistently anticipate and meet the child's needs before she experiences any discomfort. Therefore, the child does not experience any sense of need and the cycle is disrupted.

✔ The child experiences the loss of the primary caregiver either physically or emotionally (e.g., mother is depressed, hospitalized, dies, or the child is removed from the home).

✔ The child experiences frequent disruptions in care, which does not allow him to develop a specific bond. Due to parental career changes, Jason was in three different child care centers his first year of life. Now three, he has been labeled hyperactive. When he experiences frustration, he throws temper tantrums and will bite other children to insure he gets the toy he wants and ultimately the attention he needs.

✔ Prolonged or repeated separations of the infant from his/her primary caregiver during the first three years of life may result in a break in attachment. The following chart shows the length of separation time that may produce disruption of the bonding process.

Age of Child	When Damage May Occur
1. Birth to 2 years old	After 3 days
2. 2 to 5 years old	After 2 months
3. School age	After 6 months
4. Older school age	After 1 year

A break in the attachment process may impact the overall level of attachment experienced by the infant or toddler.

Level of Attachment

Attachment is not an either/or issue. Attachment can be viewed on a continuum from "extremely bonded" to "extremely unattached." For our purposes the following four levels of attachments will be utilized:

1. **Securely attached.** These children feel confident that their parent figures will provide comfort and assistance when needed. This trust allows children to explore and interact with the world around them. Parents report that children are relatively easy to console and able to both give and receive affection.

2. **Insecurely attached.** These children are not sure that their parent figures will take care of them. They are more likely to experience severe separation anxiety, to be clinging and less willing to explore their worlds. These children are ambivalent, wanting their parents but sometimes simultaneously resisting their touch, love, and affection.

3. **Poorly attached.** These children have no confidence that they will receive care when they seek it. In fact, these children expect to be rejected. They will try to live their lives without love and support by becoming emotionally self-sufficient. In most cases they will not be able to give or receive love and affection.

4. **Unattached.** These children are the most difficult because they do not belong to anyone. They are like "lost souls" and grow up with limited understanding of cause and effect. These children do not give or accept love.

Recognizing Children with Attachment Problems

One of the challenges facing teachers and parents today is how to recognize a child with attachment problems. These children exhibit identifiable patterns of behavior, some of which include:

1. **Poor Eye Contact.** Children who missed early interactions (like peek-a-boo) with their caregivers are not programmed to look at faces or make eye contact in order to read social cues. In abusive families, where control is an issue, eye contact is discouraged or punished because parents interpret it as an attempt by the child to be controlling. Abused children learn to observe their surroundings by means of sidelong glances, using their peripheral vision.

2. **Withdrawal.** Withdrawal can take several forms. The child can actually withdraw physically (pull away from the group, run away, pretend to sleep). The child may withdraw emotionally by pulling away from hugs or cringe as though she were afraid when an adult comes near. The child indicates that she doesn't want to be close or held. The adult generally tends to stay away to keep from frightening or disturbing the child.

3. **Chronic Anxiety.** Children with attachment problems tend to be very fearful that the parent figure won't be there for them when they need care or comfort. This is especially true of children who have had abrupt changes in their lives. They are generally possessive, clinging, and fearful of being abandoned. You may see behaviors such as nail biting and other forms of fidgeting.

4. **Aggressive and/or hyperactive.** It is very difficult to get close to a child

who is kicking, hitting, biting, or moving all the time. Most adults give up after awhile. The child is successful at keeping the adult at a distance so he will not be hurt physically or psychologically. The child has unresolved anxiety, anger, and rage, which is displayed in his daily environment.

5. **Indiscriminate Affection.** These children may respond inappropriately and affectionately to strangers. Their affection is often phony and insincere. They are as likely to respond to a stranger with the same hugs, touching, and enthusiasm as you would expect them to direct toward their own parents or caregivers. These children generally have few friends and take up with strangers in an attempt to fill a void of companionship.

6. **Over-competency.** Many of these children insist on doing everything for themselves. They appear not to need parenting. When they do need help, they grant permission to the adult to help them by saying, "You may button my dress." At other times, however, they will appear less mature than their age, especially when they are feeling frustrated. Their outward behavior at times sends the message of being self-reliant, independent, and not needing help.

7. **Lack of Self-Awareness.** In abusive or neglectful families or environments, the child does not learn to recognize certain kinds of discomfort and associate it with what brings relief. As a result, these children tend to lack awareness of their own bodies. They may overeat, wet the bed, and soil themselves. They may be unaware of extreme temperatures and often do not react to pain. Sometimes they inflict injury on themselves.

8. **Control Battles.** These children constantly test the limits placed on them by others. Outwardly, they appear to need to be in control, while inside they feel insecure and out of control. They are often labeled immature, emotionally disturbed, or learning disabled. They frequently use manipulation, opposition, or disruption as a means of control. They may also control by acting withdrawn and helpless. The key point is that the child expends a great deal

of energy trying to keep the world working on her agenda.

9. **Delayed Moral Development.** These children are not motivated to please or understand others. They seek only to please themselves in a frantic attempt to get their needs met. They are sometimes cruel to animals and other children. They lie and steal, and when caught, have little or no remorse. They may deny their action in spite of overwhelming evidence. Stealing, hoarding, and gorging food are common among these children. They have a constant feeling of emptiness that they seek to fill with food.

10. **Cognitive Dysfunction.** A child who has had a break in the attachment process will have difficulties with cause and effect thinking. Without an understanding of cause and effect, thinking is distorted. These children may exhibit signs of speech pathology and learning disabilities. Upon evaluation, they may be diagnosed with minimal brain dysfunction. Lack of adequate caregiving (both prenatal and postnatal) prohibits the child's nervous system from organizing in an efficient manner. The child may be hyperactive, easily distracted, impulsive, subject to emotional ups and downs, and may overreact to many of life's natural highs and lows.

"Strong emotional bonding between caregiver and infant lays the foundation for healthy psychological, physical, and cognitive development."

Children with attachment problems can be helped to redefine themselves and the world around them through the *I Love You Rituals*. Moving from a view of oneself as not lovable to lovable requires the unconditional experiences presented in the *I Love You Rituals*. Changing the view of the world from a scary place to a safe place requires an adult willing to commit time and attention to a child. As the relationship between the child and the adult grows through the *I Love You Rituals*, trust is developed. This trust is then internalized, and the view of the world is changed. All children need somebody to accept them unconditionally. You could be the person that literally breathes life into a drowning child.

I Love You Rituals and Children with Attachment Problems

I Love You Rituals are modeled after the social games parents play with infants. A social game is defined as a game in which two people are interacting together to produce possible continued interaction. Notice the level of uncertainty that exists within a social game. As a player you never really know what will happen: will the interaction produce a response from the child, will the interactions be sustained, or will the game be maintained? This level of uncertainty is the risk factor. Some children who have experienced a great deal of uncertainty in their lives react to this uncertainty with anxiety. Adults can feel the same way. What is important to remember is the value of these types of interactions for children who have not had their needs met. Understanding the value helps adults continue to play the games with children who seem at first not to be enjoying them.

In addition to the general purposes *I Love You Rituals* serve for all children, these interactions can help children who are hurting in the following very significant ways:

1. **Keep the child at an optimal level of arousal.** Have you noticed some children have trouble modulating their arousal system? They are easily upset and once frustrated, they have a very difficult time regaining their composure. *I*

Love You Rituals are designed to build relationships that help children internalize or adjust their arousal system to a more even temperament.

2. **Provide the child with a feeling of control over the environment, which fosters self-confidence and promotes intellectual growth.** Have you noticed some children seem to lack a feeling of control and are always seeking to gain control over others, situations, or events? *I Love You Rituals* provide a relationship based on an integrated dance of responsiveness. As the adult is responsive to the child, the child learns to become responsive to others. In this dance the child learns a feeling of control that comes from within, not from controlling outside events.

3. **Expose the child to intense social interactions, which promote attachment and provide the basis of all other social and communication skills.** Have you noticed that some children are missing the skills of successfully being able to get along with other children? They have trouble making and sustaining friends, taking turns, and sharing. *I Love You Rituals* are games involving a dance of responsiveness that becomes the platform from which turntaking and sharing evolve.

4. **Encourage the child to engage her surroundings.** Have you noticed some children have stereotypical play? They tend to play the same thing repeatedly, or they have trouble getting involved in play and tend to move impulsively from toy to toy without truly getting involved. *I Love You Rituals* allow the child to experience successful engagement with a caring adult. The adult directs the game, extending the child's abilities to attend and focus.

5. **Cause the child to attend more closely to the social aspects of language.** Have you noticed that a significant number of children who hurt have language and speech delays? *I Love You Rituals* are generally face-oriented games. The games increase the child's ability to focus on the face of the adult. With this focus, the child becomes more attuned to the part of the body that produces speech.

CHAPTER 3

Getting Started And Insuring Success

"These are only hints and guesses, hints followed by guesses; and the rest is prayer, observance, discipline, thought and action."

— T.S. Eliot

I Love You Rituals are designed to communicate love to the child. Many of us have heard comments such as, "Yes, I love you. Now go play." The words were there but something was missing. Love says, "I rejoice in your presence, I affirm your value, and I let my thoughts of you grow, change, and evolve." It is crucial that the relationship you build with the child during the *I Love You Rituals* is a loving relationship. In order to insure the games indeed are loving, you must do two things.

1. **Be fully present with the child.** This sounds wonderful in writing and this is our goal, but how do we do this? To be fully present one must choose to do certain things.

    Be in the moment. Simply stated, your mind must be clear of clutter. You cannot be thinking about what to cook for dinner, when you will vacuum, or what is the next line in the rhyme. You cannot be thinking of how to get the lunch count in, whose job it is to feed the hamsters, or if you are doing this right. The clutter in your mind takes you out of the moment. Children can sense this psychological leaving and generally think they caused it. The message then received from the child's point of view is not "I am loved" but "I am not worth being with."

    See yourself and the child as complete, good enough, and totally deserving. Do whatever it takes to remove all doubt in yourself and the child for these few minutes. If needed, pretend you are the perfect parent with the perfect child. Teachers can pretend that for the next few moments, whatever happens is exactly as it should be. This includes the time you forget the rhyme. If you forget a part of the interaction, move on or make up something new.

    Be accepting. If for any reason you find yourself feeling annoyed or upset while playing, stop the game. A feeling of upset is a signal to you that the child is not meeting some expectation you have of him or her. You had an image in your head of how the game was supposed to be played and now it is going a little differently than you had planned. In these *I Love You Rituals*, the goal is not to have the child meet your expectations. The goal is to join in play to experience total acceptance.

2. **Remember your purpose.** The goal of joining with the child in these delightful experiences is to rejoice in togetherness, experience the beauty of each other, and delight in the expression of love that we all are. Relax, have fun, cry, giggle, sing, just be yourself - begin to trust, all is well.

Steps to Playing I Love You Rituals

Step 1: Read the game. Make sure you understand the game itself. If the game involves a rhyme, learn it.

Step 2: Select a time and a place to engage in your rituals. Many children enjoy knowing when and where they will receive your undivided attention. If you are a school teacher, two or three ritual times are suggested per day. It is most important to provide the child with an I Love You Ritual first thing in the morning. You then may want to give a booster shot of focused attention midday (naptime) and when the child leaves school. For parents at home, a morning and an evening ritual begin and end the day on a wonderful note.

Step 3: Be responsive to the child's cues. You may start to play one game and the next thing you know, you and the child have created an entirely new game. These games are not written in stone; they were made up. You can do the same thing. These are some common child-initiated cues you might see:

Hide-and-seek or peek-a-boo. If the child starts a hiding or peek-a-boo game, this might mean the child is saying, "You can't see me; do you care? Will you look for me? Am I important enough to find?" This also puts the child in control of when to be found, which reduces some of the child's anxiety.

Chase me. Hopefully the child will not be able to get away from you to start this game; however, you never know. The meaning of this is similar, "Do you like me enough to come after me? Did you notice I was gone? Will you miss me if I am gone?" Again, this gives the child a bit of control as to when to be caught. Your response to the child is to catch him or her and say, "I got you. You ran off and I came after you. I won't let you leave me. It is our time to play and I love being with you."

Playing baby games. Sometimes the child will suggest a game that puts him in the role of a baby. This may indicate that the child trusts you to care for him. He feels safe enough to let down his guard - it is nice to be held and relaxed, and not to have to be a certain way to please others. Your response is to rock, sing, and take care of the child, regardless of age, like he was a baby.

Playing asleep. This may indicate one of two things. First, the child might be saying, "I feel comfortable and relaxed with you; safe enough just to nod out." Or the child may be trying to control the situation and may be communicating: "This is very frightening for me. I am scared this will not last. This is too overwhelming for me. Will you go away if I go away?" The response is to stay engaged with the child. Do not leave the child. You might choose to rock and sing to the child.

Stealing body parts. If the child begins to steal some of your body parts (like the "I got your nose game"), it might be an indication that the child likes you enough to want to be a part of you. "Is it okay that I like you this much?" might be the message of the interaction. Your response is to play the game. You might say, "You got my nose. Where is my nose? I can't smell."

Reaching out and touching the adult. When the child starts initiating touch to you, it is a statement that you are becoming real to the child. The child has been seen enough and is starting to be able to "see" others. The child is feeling safe with you. Your response is to let the child know you appreciate the contact. You can do this verbally and nonverbally. You might say, "You walked over and touched my hair. I really liked that."

Beginning a game you have played in the past. When the child brings up past games to play, she is saying, "I care about what we have done together. Our time of play is important to me and I remember it well. I have had fun and I want it to continue." Your response is to be willing and receptive to the child's suggestions. You might say, "I remember that game too, or "I enjoyed playing that game with you also."

Step 4: Be conscious of the difference between child initiative and child control. Sometimes children offer ideas to control the relationship and sometimes they offer ideas to contribute to the relationship. Intuitively, you will know the difference. You are in charge. Do not let the child control you. If a child says, "We are going to play _____ and it goes like this," you might respond, "That is a wonderful idea. Here is the game we will be playing." Gently and in a playful manner, get the lead back from the child and proceed with the game.

Step 5: Relax and have fun. Never make yourself or the child wrong. These games cannot be wrong and neither can you.

Elements to Remember When Playing with Children Who Are Hurting

1. The adult is in charge. The adult is the leader in these games. These games are modeled after parent-infant interactions and require the partners to engage in a dance, with the adult always being the leader. It would seem silly for a parent to look at her four-month-old baby and ask, "What will we play or how will we play this game?" The adult initiates the interactions and continues with delight as long as the interaction is sustained. Being in charge requires the adult to stay engaged with the child, regardless of the child's response.

2. Have fun. Each activity, whether the child resists or not, is surrounded in playfulness and fun. When an infant struggles as you are trying to dress him or her, a responsible parent tries to make a game out of it by singing, tickling, soothing, or making sounds with the movement. Getting mad at the infant's resistance to getting dressed does nothing but weaken the trust of the infant and the safety of the relationship. The same is true for these *I Love You Rituals*. Some children may resist having fun. The role of the adult is to seduce them out of their control and into engagement. This is done by the adult continuing to be a playful person, regardless of the child's responses.

3. No hurts. The adult, while in charge, must create an atmosphere of safety and nurturance. The games require caring, gentle touch. No hitting or hurts of any kind are allowed. If a child should strike out at the adult, stop the hit if possible and state, "No hurts. I will not hurt you and I will not let you hurt me." Once the limit is stated, continue with the game.

4. Stick together. Keep close to the child. These interactions are very intimate, loving games. Sometimes you might think, "This child could do this without me." Indeed he or she could; however, the point of the interaction would be lost.

Playing with Children Who Are Hurting

These games are essential for children who are hurting. However, there are some guidelines that need to be followed to insure success.

✔ **Touch children firmly.** Some children who are hurting have had assaults to their body. Their skin sensory organ can be either hyper or hyposensitive. Stop reading this book. Take one of your hands and grasp your other forearm. Remove your hand. Can you still feel a lingering presence of where your hand used to be? That is about the firmness you will want to use. Remember to be sensitive to the cues of the child.

✔ **Touch children mainly on their extremities.** Most of the *I Love You Rituals* involve touching children on their hands. Some of the interactions require touching the child's face. For children who are hurting, abrupt or sudden movements to the face are scary. In general, it is best to stay away from the face and the stomach area in the beginning. As the relationship grows and trust develops, you can then proceed to touch these more vulnerable spaces. Rituals that may be scary for children are noted in the directions for playing that game.

✔ **Do not tickle.** Tickling can easily cross the line between fun and a form of aggression. Many of us have experienced this phenomenon as children ourselves. For children who are hurting, do not tickle. For children who are not hurting, be sensitive to how much is too much.

✔ **If it doesn't feel right, don't do it.** Use your intuition. If you have concerns about a game, don't play it.

✔ **If you need permission, get it.** If you work in a school, talk to the child's parents. Let the parents and administration know what you are doing. Invite them to share in the development and exchange of rituals. Talk to people; share what you are doing.

✔ **Do not give up on the child.** The child may be resistive at first. Continue to be playful and caring. Do not let the child's response push you away. He or she is testing you: "Are you going to be like everyone else and reject me?" By your actions you will be answering, "No."

CHAPTER 4

Positive Nursery Rhymes

"If we don't change our direction,
we are likely to end up
where we are headed."

— Ancient Chinese Proverb

A Wonderful Woman Who Lived in a Shoe

A wonderful woman lived in a shoe.
She had so many children
She knew exactly what to do.
She held them,
She rocked them,
And tucked them in bed.
"I love you, I love you"
Is what she said.

Preparation and Instructions: This is a wonderful poem to do with your children at naptime or bedtime. Have the child sit in your lap or lean against your body. Wrap your arms around the child and hold on to one hand.

"A wonderful woman lived in a shoe."

Get in ready position during this line by having the child's hands facing you, palms out.

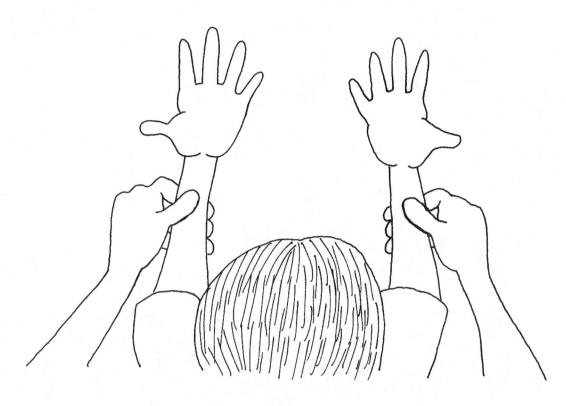

"She had so many children"

Touch each finger on one hand as you say a word from this line.

"She knew exactly what to do."

Begin touching the fingers of the other hand. This time there are six words and five fingers. When you say the rhyme, say one word per finger except for "to do." Say those together on the last finger.

"She held them,"

Fold the child's fingers into a fist and put both your hands around the child's hand. This is like swaddling the child's hand with your hands.

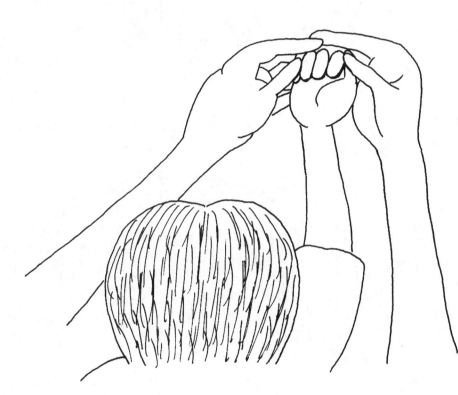

"She rocked them,"

Holding the child's hand securely, rock it side to side.

"And tucked them in bed."

Put the child's hand close against his or her chest. This will place you in a slight hugging position.

"'I love you, I love you' is what she said."

Say these words lovingly to the child as you continue to hold her or him.

Peter Peter Pumpkin Eater

Peter Peter Pumpkin Eater,
Had a friend he loved to greet.
Treated her (him) with kind respect,
And in the morning hugged her (his) neck.

Preparation and Instructions: Stand or kneel facing the child.

"Peter Peter Pumpkin Eater,"

With delight in your facial expression, and at eye level with the child, say the line.

"Had a friend he loved to greet."

Reach out and shake the hand of the child.

"Treated her (him) with kind respect,"

Gently put your left arm on the child's right shoulder and demonstrate a very kind touch.

"And in the morning hugged her (his) neck."

Move into a gentle hug from this position.

Twinkle Twinkle, Little Star

Twinkle twinkle, little star,

What a wonderful child you are!

With bright eyes and nice round cheeks,

Talented person from head to feet.

Twinkle twinkle, little star,

What a wonderful child you are!

Preparation and Instructions: It is important that you be similar heights for this activity. You may choose to stand, kneel, or sit with the child in order to obtain this position.

"Twinkle twinkle, little star,"

Hold the child's hands and raise them slightly above your heads. Wiggle your fingers together for the "twinkle" representation of stars.

"What a wonderful child you are!"

Bring your arms down and rest your hands on the child's shoulders and the child will have his hands on your shoulders.

"With bright eyes and nice round cheeks,"

The adult takes both hands off the shoulders and touches the child's face with both pointer fingers. First, touch the child next to his eyes and then bring the fingers down around the child's cheeks. If the child seems to withdraw as you touch his face, just pretend to touch these parts.

"Talented person from head to feet."

Take the child's hands in yours and put them up high (from head) and take them down low (to feet).

"Twinkle twinkle, little star,"

Take the arms back up to the sky like in the beginning. Wiggle the fingers to represent the shining stars.

"What a wonderful child you are!"

End the interaction with a hug.

Little Miss Muffet

Little Miss Muffet sat on her tuffet,

Eating her curds and whey.

Along came a spider and sat down beside her,

And said, "Have a good day!"

Preparation and Instructions: Explain to the child that a tuffet is a little chair. Both you and the child will each make a tuffet by making a fist with one of your hands. Place your tuffets together with knuckles touching. Tell the child that with your non-tuffet hand you will be Miss Muffet and he or she will be the spider. Continue your actions as described below.

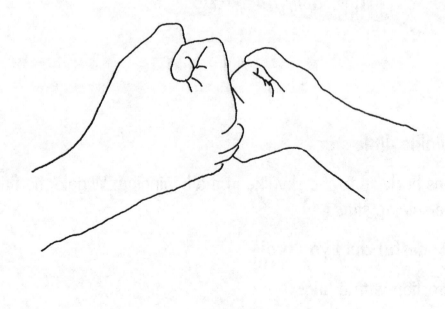

"Little Miss Muffet sat on her tuffet,"

With your non-tuffet hand, make Little Miss Muffet by holding up two fingers from a fist. While saying the words in the rhyme above, bring Miss Muffet over and have her sit on your other hand or tuffet.

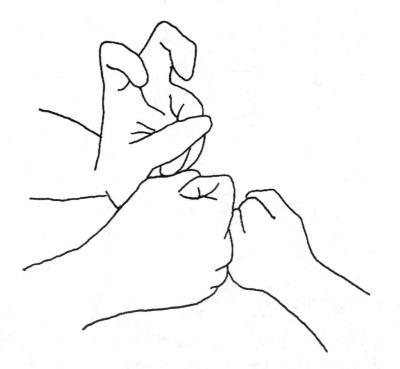

"Eating her curds and whey."

The two upright fingers will move back and forth as in an eating motion.

"Along came a spider and sat down beside her,"

The child will use his non-tuffet hand as a spider. Holding the hand palm down with fingers dangling down like a spider, the child walks the spider over and sits it on his tuffet hand.

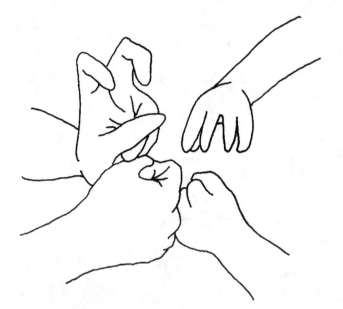

"And said, "Have a good day!"

The adult then uses her own Little Miss Muffet hand to open the tuffet hand of the child and shakes his hand while lovingly stating, "Have a good day!"

Humpty Dumpty

Humpty Dumpty sat on the wall.
Humpty Dumpty had a great fall.
All the Queen's horses and All the King's men,
Could put Humpty together again.

Preparation and Instructions: In this game the adult is the wall and the child is Humpty Dumpty. Each line of the rhyme requires the adult to interact and guide the child.

Beginning Position: The wall is created by the adult holding her hands out in front of her, palms facing her own body, and her thumbs pointing up and extended 90 degrees from the fingers. The finger tips of each hand should be touching. The two Humpty Dumptys are made by the child closing each hand into a fist. The balled fists represent eggs.

"Humpty Dumpty sat on the wall."

The adult holds up her wall and the child places his or her two fists on top of the wall as shown in the picture above. The adult says the first line of the rhyme.

"Humpty Dumpty had a great fall."

The adult changes her hands from the wall position and holds onto the arms (about at the wrist of the child) of the two Humpty Dumptys as they fall down to each side of the child. (It is important to hold onto the child at all times, sending the message, "You have fallen, but I am here for you.")

"All the Queen's horses and"

During this line, the adult releases the child's wrists, moves her hands up the child's arms just below the elbow, and gives the child's arms a gentle, yet firm squeeze.

"All the King's men,"

The adult releases the child from this squeeze, moves both hands down the child's arms until slightly above the wrist, and again gives the child a gentle, yet firm squeeze.

"Could put Humpty together again."

The adult brings the child's hands together so that one of the child's fists wraps around the other fist. Simultaneously, the adult takes her two hands and wraps them securely around both of the child's hands. You want to give the impression that the adult's hands are wrapped around the child's hands, like a blanket would wrap a newborn baby snugly in your arms. The adult then brings all the united hands to the eye level of the child while saying the last line.

Georgie Porgie

Georgie Porgie, pudding and pie,
Gave his friend a big High Five!
With his friend he loved to play,
A gift of a smile he gave each day.

Preparation and Instructions: This poem provides the opportunity to expand the concept of gifts with children. True gifts are the love we share with each other, not the material goods. The children learn that smiling is a gift of joy to be treasured. As you expand on this rhyme, you can ask the children to name other "gifts" that can be given and insert them in the poem (e.g., a gift of "a hug" or "a wink" she gave each day). Other possible gifts include pinky hugs (little fingers intertwine), thumb touches, and a kiss (blow a kiss).

Georgie Porgie, pudding and pie,"

Stand or sit facing the child, making eye contact as you say this first line. Move your shoulders up and down to the rhythm of the words.

"Gave his friend a big High Five!"

With both hands execute a loving, gentle High Five with the child.

"With his friend he loved to play,"

Holding your hands out in front of you with your fingers pointing up and palms facing the child, wiggle your fingers with delight and touch the wiggling fingers of the child. This is a fast, happy motion as if you were tickling each other's fingers in the air. Be sure to make contact while celebrating this motion.

"A gift of a smile he gave each day."

Make a wonderful smile. Put your hands up to your face, and use them to frame a smile to the child.

Margie Pargie

Margie Pargie, pudding and pie,

Gave her friend a big High Five!

With her friend she loved to play,

A gift of a handshake she gave each day.

Preparation and Instructions: Margie Pargie is conducted in the exact same manner as Georgie Porgie (see page 60), except the gift given at the end is a handshake instead of a smile.

Think of all the gifts you can give today!

62

Mary Had a Little Lamb

Mary had a little lamb whose fleece was white as snow.
Everywhere that Mary went the lamb was sure to go.
It followed her to school one day; everything was new.
The children were surprised to see the lamb was really you!

Preparation and Instructions: You will need a white sock for this game. Standing or sitting face to face, the adult introduces herself as Mary before beginning the rhyme. This is done by waving hello with a hand and saying, "Hello. It is wonderful to see you. My name is Mary. I am looking for a lamb to play with. I think I see one!" (Look directly at one of the child's hands.) You are ready to begin the rhyme.

"Mary had a little lamb whose fleece was white as snow."

While saying this line, put the white sock on one of the child's hands.

"Everywhere that Mary went the lamb was sure to go."

Put the hand that you introduced as Mary on the "lamb" (child's hand covered with sock). Move both hands around, making sure both hands stay connected together.

"It followed her to school one day; everything was new."

Continue to move both hands up and down and all around in this mirror play fashion.

"The children were surprised to see the lamb was really you!"

Pull the sock off the child's hand and look surprised and delighted.

Message of the Game: The message of this game is "I will stay with you no matter what you do or where you go. I am here for you." Because of this message, many children will test to see if you really mean what you say. They will do the testing by making it difficult for your hands to stay with theirs. Some children will hide their hands or run away to begin a game of Hide and Seek. If the child refuses to stay connected and gets away from you, go into the version of Little Bo Peep described on the next page.

Little Bo Peep

Little Bo Peep has lost her sheep
And doesn't know where to find them.
She'll look for them and bring them home
Staying always close beside them.

Preparation and Instructions: This game can be played as an extension of Mary Had a Little Lamb or played in isolation.

"Little Bo Peep has lost her sheep"

As you say this line, in a sad voice, have your hands begin to look for the child's hands. If you are playing this game as an extension of Mary Had a Little Lamb, more than likely the child is hiding his hands or has actually run off to play Hide and Seek. If you are playing this game as a solo, the child's hands will not be hidden, so you can look right at one of them.

"And doesn't know where to find them."

Make an exaggerated facial expression that displays confusion and sadness. Then make a questioning face as if to say, "Where could they be?" If the child has run off or continues to hide his hands, you can become very sad. You may want to repeat this line and begin a pretend cry. This sends a message to the child, "I feel sad. I miss you. I hope your hands come back and play."

"She'll look for them and bring them home,"

Look all around for the child's hands, especially in silly places(regardless of whether they are still hidden or not). Look in the child's ears, under the sleeve of his shirt, and in his sock or shoe.

"Staying always close beside them."

Once you find the child's hands, give the whole child a loving hug. If the child continues to hide his hands, simply end the rhyme with your hands near the child's hands.

Hot Cross Buns

Hot cross buns, hot cross buns,

One penny, two penny

Hot cross buns!

Give them to your daughters;

give them to your sons.

One penny, two penny

Hot cross buns!

Preparation and Instructions: This poem has slightly more difficult hand motions than the previous games. Young children (4-5 years) will be more successful if you teach the hand clapping first without any words. Once they have the clapping down, then you are ready for words and actions. Older children will have no trouble learning the words and actions simultaneously. Sit facing the child. Give the child a signal to begin the game. Say, "Ready, set, go!"

"Hot cross buns, hot cross buns"

Each clap is made in timing with the words. When you say "Hot," clap your thighs with both hands, "Cross," clap your hands together, and "Buns," clap the child's hands. The child is to conduct the same clapping pattern as the adult.

"One penny, two penny"

Both the adult and child hold up one finger (pointer finger) on their right hands and two fingers (pointer and tall finger) on their left hands. The adult and child touch one finger on their right hands together while saying "One Penny." Next touch the two fingers of the left hands together and say "Two Penny."

"Hot cross buns!"

Repeat the clapping of hands as when you began.

"Give them to your daughters; Give them to your sons."

When you say "Give them to your daughters," take your right hand and shake hands with the child's right hand. When you say "Give them to your sons," take your left hand and shake hands with the child's left hand.

"One penny, two penny"

Repeat the finger touches as before.

"Hot cross buns!"

End the interaction with a final series of hand claps as done before.

Mary Mary Extraordinary

Mary Mary (Jerry Jerry) Extraordinary,
How do your fingers grow?
With fingernails and no tails,
And a High Five to go.

Preparation and Instructions: Stand facing the child. Depending on his/her size, you may need to kneel to be at a working level. You and the child ball your hands into fists. Both of you put your fists out front touching each other.

"Mary Mary (Jerry Jerry) Extraordinary,"

The adult and child stand with their hands touching in the beginning position as indicated above. The adult may either use a female or male name for the game.

"How do your fingers grow?"

When this is said, you and the child spring your fingers up from a closed fist position to an extended open position. Now your palms are touching the palms of the child.

"With fingernails and no tails,"

When you speak the word "fingernails," both of you wiggle your fingers. When you say "no tails," both of you wiggle your "behinds" as if they are tails.

"And a High Five to go."

Give an enthusiastic High Five!

Note: For "Jerry Jerry Extraordinary," conduct it in the same fashion as described above, except at the end give a Low Five.

To Market, to Market

To market, to market, to buy a fat pig.
Home again, home again, jiggity jig.
To market, to market, to buy a fat hog.
Home again, home again, jiggity jog.
To market, to market, to buy a new gown.
Home again, home again.
Whoops! the horse fell down.

Preparation and Instructions: This is a game with an element of risk (falling or being hurt). Children who have had their needs met enjoy these games. Children who have been hurt may find these games anxiety producing. In their anxiety they may do a number of things. Some children will try to make the game rougher and more dangerous, actually creating a situation where you may find it hard to keep the game safe. Some children may become limp like a noodle. Others may go along with you, but they appear to find no joy in the activity. Play this game gently with impulsive children who have a tendency to fly off the handle. You control the pace and the roughness of the horse - do not let the child. Also if you suspect a child has been sexually abused, do not play this game at all. Start the game by having the child say, "Giddy-up!" This lets him or her know when the movement will begin and reduces anxiety.

"To market, to market, to buy a fat pig. Home again, home again, jiggity jig."

Have the child sit on your lap facing you with his or her legs straddling your legs. Gently bounce the child as if he or she is riding a pony to the market.

"To market, to market, to buy a fat hog. Home again, home again, jiggity jog."

Repeat the action. Vary the intensity depending on the child. (See notes above.)

"To market, to market, to buy a new gown. Home again, home again."

Continue with the horsey ride, holding onto both of the child's hands with a firm grip.

"Whoops! the horse fell down."

Spread your legs and let the rider (child) fall gently through your legs as you support and catch the child.

Wee Willie (Wendy) Winkie

Wee Willie (Wendy) Winkie runs through the town,
Upstairs and downstairs in his (her) nightgown.
Rapping at the window,
Looking through the lock.
"Are the children in their beds?
For now it's eight o'clock."

Preparation and Instructions: The ending of this poem provides you with many opportunities. You can vary the time of day used to go with your schedule. At times you may want to change the question entirely. You could say, "Are the children in their seats, for now it's one o'clock?"Stand (sit) facing the child to begin the poem and hold the child's hand with the palm face up.

"Wee Willie (Wendy) Winkie runs through the town,"

Holding the palm of the child's hand, place two fingers from your other hand on the child's palm. Have the two fingers move up and down on the palm, as if they are warming up to run in a race.

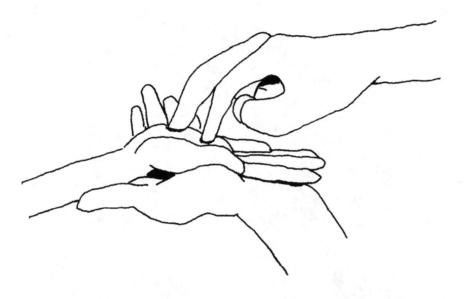

"Upstairs and downstairs in his (her) nightgown."

Run the two fingers up to the child's elbow and back down to the child's hand. Go up on the word "upstairs" and down on the word "downstairs." When you say "in his nightgown," make a surprised look on your face.

"Rapping at the window,"

Make each hand into a fist like you would be knocking at the door, and gently tap the child on each side of his or her head four times.

"Looking through the lock."

Cover the child's eyes with your hands as if to play peek-a-boo. Then open your hands to see the child. As you open your hands, move up close to the face of the child.

"'Are the children in their beds?'"

With your hands opened over the eyes, your head very close to the child's face, and with a stern, curious, facial expression, ask, "Are the children in their beds?"

"'For now it's eight o'clock.'"

Remove your hands and point to your wristwatch. If you do not have a watch, point to a clock on the wall or counter.

Jack Be Noodle

Jack be Noodle,
Jack be stiff,
Jack come over and hug me quick.

Preparation and Instructions: Perform Jack Be Noodle three times using three different body parts of the child. Begin with the pointer finger, then use the whole hand, and finish by using the child's entire arm.

"Jack be noodle,"

Stand (or kneel) facing the child and hold the child's pointer finger. As you say "Jack be Noodle," wiggle the child's pointer finger as to make it loose and floppy.

"Jack be stiff,"

When these words are spoken, move your fingers over the child's finger to make it stiff.

"Jack come over and hug me quick."

Lock your pointer finger with the child's pointer finger as if to do a finger hug.

"Jack be noodle,"

Repeat the above actions using the child's entire hand. Hold the child's wrist and have the hand be floppy.

77

"Jack be stiff,"

This time help the child make a stiff hand.

"Jack come over and hug me quick."

This is a handshake between the two of you.

"Jack be noodle,"

Repeat the above actions and words using the child's entire arm from the shoulder down.

"Jack be stiff,"

Help the child make a stiff arm.

"Jack come over and hug me quick."

Give the child a hug.

CHAPTER 5

Interactive Finger Plays

"Together we're better!"

— Bev Bos

Dancing Hands

____child's name____'s hands are up and

____child's name____'s hands are down.

____child's name____'s hands are dancing

All around the town.

Dancing on my knees,

Dancing on my feet,

Dancing on my shoulders,

And dancing on my cheeks (blow raspberries).

____child's name____'s hands are up and

____child's name____'s hands are down.

____child's name____'s hands are dancing

All around the town.

Dancing on your knees,

Dancing on your feet,

Dancing on your shoulders,

And dancing on your cheeks (blow raspberries).

Preparation and Instructions: This interaction has two verses. On the first verse move the child's hands and have him touch your body parts as they are named. On the second verse move the child's hands and have the child touch himself. (Because of the intrusiveness of the ending, it is important that you do this to yourself first. This will reduce the anxiety some children might experience.)

"___child's name___'s hands are up and"

Holding both of the child's hands close to the wrist, flip the hands so the fingers point

"___child's name___'s hands are down."

Flip the fingers down.

"___child's name___'s hands are dancing"

Move the hands around in the air.

"All around the town."

Continue to move the child's hands in the air.

"Dancing on my knees,"

Holding the child's hands, guide them to pat on your knees.

"Dancing on my feet,"

Guide the child's hands to pat on your feet.

"Dancing on my shoulders,"

Continue to your shoulders.

"And dancing on my cheeks."

Bring the child's hands up to your face and at the same time fill your cheeks with air. Guide the child's hands to gently tap your cheeks so you *blow raspberries as the air comes out. This surprise ending is delightful for children. Remember to guide the child's hands securely so that the touch is gentle. *I Love You Rituals* are always safe, both for the child and for the adult.

Second Verse: The second verse is conducted the same as the first, except during this verse you guide the child's hand to pat his own knees, feet, shoulders, and cheeks. Hopefully, the child will fill up his cheeks with air for the finale. You may have to help some children understand their role at the end. It is crucial that you be the guide of the child's hands so they can learn how to touch others gently. Children who have not been touched gently must learn from someone. Never let a child hurt himself or you during an interaction.

* Blowing raspberries is an old-time children's favorite. It occurs when the cheeks are filled with air, and then the adult or child gently touches the cheeks and a squirt of air is forced out of the mouth making a funny noise.

Five Little Babies

One little baby
Rocking in a tree,
Two little babies
Looking at me.
Three little babies
Crawling on the floor,
Four little babies
Knocking on the door.
Five little babies,
Playing hide and seek.
Don't look, don't look
Until I say . . . PEEK!

Preparation and Instructions: Sit with the child on your lap facing you or on the floor so you are face to face. Select one of the child's hands and have her extend her fingers.

"One little baby"

The adult extends her own fingers and thumb, touching them to the child's fingers and thumb three times in rhythm with the words.

"Rocking in a tree,"

Lay the child's hand across the adult's cradled hands and rock the hand as if it were a baby doll.

"Two little babies"

Hold the child's hand and put up two of the child's fingers, leaving the rest tucked.

84

"Looking at me."

Bring the child's two fingers close to your eyes as if they are pointing at your eyes.

"Three little babies"

Hold the child's hand and put up three fingers only.

"Crawling on the floor,"

Guide the child's fingers to move around on the floor, representing the crawling action.

"Four little babies"

Repeat, holding child's hand with four fingers.

"Knocking on the door."

The adult takes one of the child's hands and makes a fist. With the fist gently touch the side of the child's head. If the child seems uncomfortable with that, you can tap on a knee instead.

"Five little babies,"

Hold the child's whole hand up with extended fingers.

"Playing hide and seek."

Turn the child's hand to cover one of her eyes. Add the child's other hand so that both eyes are covered. The child may choose to peek through her hands.

"Don't look, don't look"

Keep holding the child's hands over the child's eyes. The adult moves her face slightly closer to the child.

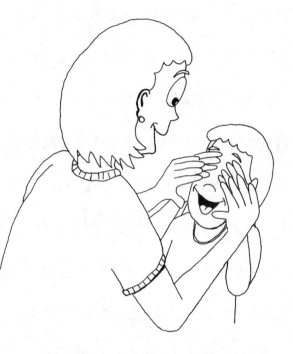

"Until I say . . . . .PEEK!"

When you say "peek," assist the child in removing her hands. Surprise the child with your smiling face.

Extensions: At the end of the poem: 1) Make an opening between the child's ring finger and middle finger. Move your face close to the child's face and as you say "peek," look through the opening. 2) Hide your face. When the hands of the child are removed for the "peek," you are not there. Immediately afterwards bring your face up to the child's and say, "Boo, I see you." 3) Make a funny face so that when the child's hands are removed, she is delightfully surprised.

Growing Up

When you were just a baby,
You did not know how to walk.
You could only crawl, crawl around like this.
When you were just a baby,
You did not know how to talk.
You could only babble, babble just like this.
Now you are this big
And go to school each day.
You can do many things
Like walk and talk and play.

Preparation and Instructions: This is a poem that gives you an opportunity to hold the child. Place the child in your lap and hold her like a baby. Many troubled children never received this type of holding and nurturing. Simply hold the child in your arms and in a soothing voice share the poem with the child.

Verse One: When you get to the end of verse one, use your hands to crawl around the child's arms and legs. Stay away from the child's stomach. This is a very vulnerable area, especially if the child has been sexually abused.

Verse Two: If you want, you can begin to talk like a baby. You can babble and coo. Stay away from crying. The child may choose to talk in baby talk. Support this process. If she chooses to "cry like a baby," your role would be that of a comforter. You might say, "The baby is upset, I will take care of her. I will keep her safe. Let me see if I can figure out what is the matter. Is she hungry? (pretend to feed) Is she sleepy? (start to rock) Does she want me to stroke her head? (begin to rub her head)

Verse Three: Trace the outline of the child's body to show just how big the child is. You could also stretch out your arms to show how long the child is. After you say all the verses, two things might happen. The child might want to show you a trick (e.g., hopping on one foot). If this is the case, admire the child's growing skills. You might comment, "You really are big! You can hop on one foot." The other thing that could happen is that the child indicates she still wants to be a baby. In this case, while you are holding, rocking, and hugging the child, say, "No matter how big we get, it still feels nice to be held and rocked."

Extension: Children love to hear stories of when they were younger or when they were a baby. The poem provides a wonderful time to share some of those cherished memories.

Here's the Beehive

Here's the beehive, where are the bees?

Hidden away where nobody sees.

Watch and you will see them come out of the hive.

One, two, three, four, five Bzzzzzzzzzzzzzzzzzzz

I'll catch them and keep them alive!

Preparation and Instructions: The child in this ritual can be sitting on your lap, sitting next to you, or both of you can be standing. Start the game with the child making a fist with his or her hand. The fist is to have the thumb tucked inside the hand. This way no "bees" are showing. Hold the child's hand in this position in one hand and manipulate the interaction with your other hand. At the end of the game when you catch the bees, stop the "Bzzzz" sound. You then may want to say, "Are they still alive?" As you open your hand and look at the child's fingers, make a "Bzzzzz" sound again. When you close your hand over the child's, stop the "Bzzzzz" noise.

"Here's the beehive, where are the bees?"

Hold the child's closed fist and look all around the hand with an inquisitive face.

90

"Hidden away where nobody sees."

Say this line with a sighing voice as you shrug your shoulders while looking at the hand.

"Watch and you will see them come out of the hive."

Light up your face with anticipation and delight and prepare your other hand to "remove the bees."

"One, two, three, four, five"

Pick out one bee at a time as you count each finger being opened.

"Bzzzzzzzz"

Once all "bees" are out, begin making a bee sound and buzz around.

"I'll catch them and keep them alive!"

Pretend to catch all the child's five fingers by tucking them inside your hand. When the "bees" are caught, stop the noise. Check on them several times to make sure they are still alive. Each checking requires a "Bzzzzz" noise.

Here's the Bunny

Here's the bunny with the ears so funny.

Here's the hole in the ground.

When a noise she hears,

She picks up her ears.

And jumps in the hole in the ground!

Preparation and Instructions: In this game the adult is the bunny and the child is the hole. The roles may change as the child becomes familiar with the game. The game can be played with the hands or with the whole body. When playing the game with the hands, the adult makes a bunny by holding up two fingers of one hand. The hole is made by circling the fingers of the child's hand as to make a zero or hole. When using the entire body, the adult makes the bunny by holding up her arms next to her head for big ears on her bunny body. The hole is made by extending both of the child's arms horizontal to the floor and connecting the hands in front of his body to form a circle.

"Here's the bunny with the ears so funny."

Hold up two fingers to show the bunny.

"Here's the hole in the ground."

The child holds up his fingers shaped like a hole.

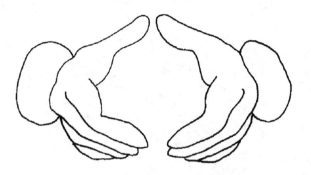

"When a noise she hears,"

The "bunny" bends her ears down by bending the two upright fingers down toward the thumb.

"She picks up her ears."

With a quick snapping motion thrust the fingers straight up in the air.

"And jumps in the hole in the ground!"

Have the two fingers jump into the "hole" provided by the child.

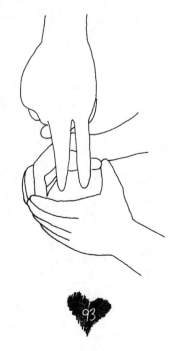

Extensions: As the big bunny goes into the arms of the hole, a hug could be given. When the little bunny jumps into the little hole, a kiss on the back of the hand can be given. The adult can kiss her own hand or the hand of the child.

Mr. Sun

Oh Mr. Sun, Sun,

Mr. Golden Sun,

Won't you smile down

On my friend __(insert child's name)__?

Oh Mr. Sun, Sun,

Mr. Golden Sun,

Won't you shine down

On my friend _____?

Materials: Face paint markers, preferably yellow and red in color.

Preparation and Instructions: This song is sung with the child while you draw a picture on the back of the child's hand. Sitting facing each other, begin the activity by holding the child's hand, with the back of the hand facing you. Have your markers or paint ready to use.

"Oh Mr. Sun, Sun,"

Draw a circle on the back of the child's hand to represent the sun.

"Mr. Golden Sun,"

From the circle draw the rays of the sun radiating outward.

"Won't you smile down"

Inside the circle draw a smiling face. Make sure the face is looking at the child and not you.

"On my friend ___(insert the child's name)___?

Show the child the drawing.

"Oh Mr. Sun, Sun,"

Trace around the circle to make it darker.

"Mr. Golden Sun,"

Trace over the sun's rays to make them darker.

"Won't you shine down"

Make the smiling face darker and more visible. You could add eye color to the face. If the child has brown eyes, make brown eyes on the sun.

"On my friend ___(insert the child's name)___?"

Extensions: Once the picture is made, you can take the child's other hand and place the child's hands back to back; the picture will transfer from one hand to the other. The child will have two pictures instead of one!

On Your Face

On your face you have a nose
And way down here you have ten toes.
Two eyes that blink,
And a head to think.

You have a chin and very near,
You have two ears to help you hear.
Arms go high and arms go low
(arms go low and arms go high).
A great big hug to say hello (say goodbye).

Preparation and Instructions: Sit in front of the child, either on the floor or in a chair. Remember your facial expressions need to be exaggerated and big with delight. For children who are hurting or for children who do not know you well, use the following: Conduct the interaction first by holding the child's hands and having the child touch you. Progress to holding the child's hands and having the child touch his own face. Finally, when the trust level has grown, you can take your hands and touch the child's face as indicated below.

"On your face you have a nose"

Touch the child's face. It is important to say the line first so the child knows what you will be doing with him. So, say the line, then touch the nose.

"And way down here you have ten toes."

Starting with your hands on the child's shoulders, slide down the child's arms and then touch or point to his toes. If the child has special needs and is sensory defensive, just point to the toes instead of sliding down the body.

"Two eyes that blink,"

Move your face closer to the child's face and blink your eyes. Encourage the child nonverbally to blink with you.

"And a head to think."

With both of your hands, gently cradle the sides of the child's head.

"You have a chin and very near,"

Touch the child's chin. Again, remember to wait until after the line is spoken so the child can anticipate the touch.

"You have two ears to help you hear."

Touch both ear lobes and whisper something short into the child's ears. Some suggestions are: "I like you, I am glad to see you, I love you, I'm glad you came to school today," etc.

"Arms go high and arms go low" (arms go low and arms go high).

Take the child's wrist and hold his arms up high over his head and back down.

"And a great big hug to say hello" (say goodbye).

Extend your arms and give the child a hug.

Extensions: The end of the activity can be changed as indicated above. If you are using this as a hello ritual, have the arms go high and then low. If you are using this as a goodbye ritual, have the arms go low and then high.

One, Two, Three, Four, Five

One, two, three, four, five,
I caught a fish alive.
Six, seven, eight, nine, ten,
I let him go again.

Why did you let him go?
Because he bit my finger so.
Which one did he bite?
The little one on the right.

Materials: Cake frosting or some kind of pudding goes well with this poem. Have a wet wipe or wet washcloth ready for clean up after the game is over.

Preparation and Instructions: Wash the child's hands.

Verse One: As you say "One, two, three, four, five," put cake frosting or pudding on the ends of the child's fingers. When you say "Six, seven, eight, nine, ten," do NOT put additional pudding or frosting on. If the child resists the frosting or the pudding, simply touch each of the child's fingers as you say "One, two, three, four, five."

Verse Two: Say this verse while holding the child's hand with pudding on the fingers. When you come to the last line, "The little one on the right," have the child lick or suck the pudding off that finger. Repeat the last two lines of the poem. "Which one did he bite? The little one on the right." Have the child lick the pudding off the next finger. Continue repeating the last two lines until all fingers are clean.

Cleaning Up: Wash the child's hands with the wet wipe or washcloth. This probably is the most important part of the game. This gives you time to nurture and care for the child. It allows you time to massage his or her hands and send the message "I will care for you" and "I am here for you." Do not rush through this wonderful moment.

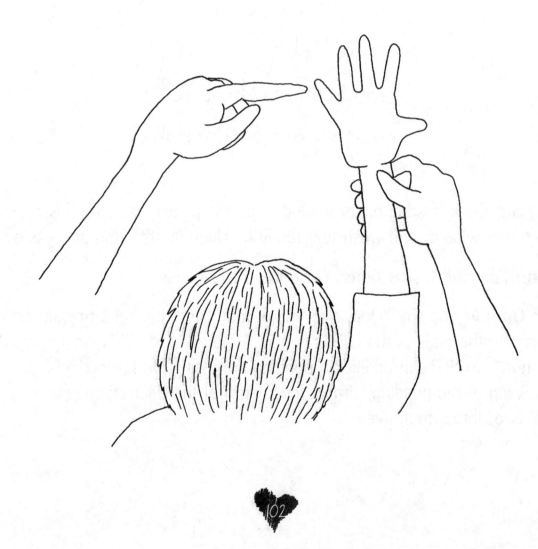

Round and Round the Garden

Round and round the garden
Goes the teddy bear.
One step, two step,
Tickle under there.

Preparation and Instructions: Begin by holding the child's hand in your hand, palm up. With the pointer finger of your other hand make circular motions in the child's palm. Originally, this was a tickle game. With children who feel safe and have had their needs met, tickle games can be fun. For children who have felt abandoned and attacked, tickle games can be scary. If you are working with a troubled child, this game must be played differently and carefully. The instructions for both types of play are provided below:

"Round and round the garden"

Draw circles on the child's hand with your pointer finger as you say, "Round and round the garden."

"Goes the teddy bear."

Continue with the circles in cadence with the chant.

"One step, two step,"

Walk your fingers up the child's arm, heading for the armpit.

"Tickle under there."

Give a gentle tickle under the child's arm.

Variation for Troubled Children: As you say "one step, two step," keep your voice calm instead of building excitement. Walk your fingers up the arm. When you say "Tickle under there," take your hand and squeeze the child's shoulder gently. As the child begins to trust you, slowly move into a more ticklish play. Go slow and be patient. The child's actions generally will tell you if he or she is anticipating fright instead of delight.

Remember, tickling can be frightening
for children who have been hurt.

There Was a Little Mouse

There was a little mouse
And she had a little house
And she lived
Up here.

Preparation and Instructions: This is the same type of game as "Round and Round the Garden." The same precautions and instructions prevail.

"There was a little mouse"

Holding the child's palm, have your fingers wiggle in his or her palm like a little mouse.

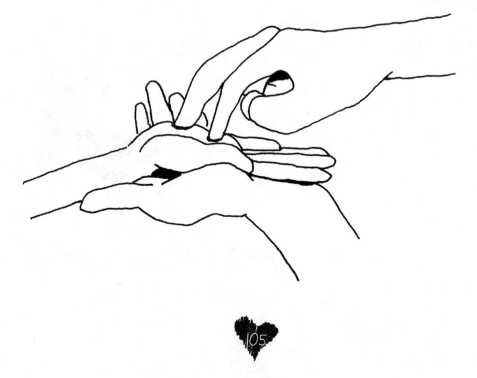

"And she had a little house"

Release the child's palm and give his or her forearm a gentle squeeze.

"And she lived"

The adult takes her hand that represents the mouse and walks up the child's palm to his or her forearm using two fingers. Simultaneously you are building anticipation of the next move with your voice tone and facial expressions.

"Up here."

Touch the child in a ticklish spot or a location that would be a surprise. This could be the ear lobe, top of the head, or the nose. Remember, for children who are hurting, tickling is perceived as just another attack.

Ten Little Candles

Ten little candles on a chocolate cake,
Whew, whew, now there are only eight.
Eight little flickers on the candlesticks,
Whew, whew, now there are only six.
Six little candles and not one more,
Whew, whew, now there are only four.
Four little candles - red, white and blue,
Whew, whew, now there are only two.
Two little candles standing in the sun,
Whew, whew, now there is none.
The chocolate cake is in my sight,
I think I'll take a little bite.

Preparation and Instructions: This delightful hand and finger interaction is great for a child's birthday. This can be done the week before the great event.

"Ten little candles on a chocolate cake,"

With your hands slightly above the wrists of the child, hold up both the child's hands, so that the child's fingers are pointing up like birthday candles on a cake.

"Whew, whew, now there are only eight."

"Blow out" (blow air out of your mouth) two of the fingers. Use enough focused blowing power so the child feels the air on his or her fingers. Simultaneously assist the child in holding those two fingers down if needed.

"Eight little flickers on the candlesticks,"

"Whew, whew, now there are only six."

"Six little candles and not one more,"

"Whew, whew, now there are only four."

"Four little candles - red, white and blue,"

"Whew, whew, now there are only two."

"Two little candles standing in the sun,"

"Whew, whew, now there is none."

Continue blowing out the candles until all candles are gone and the fingers are down.

"The chocolate cake is in my sight,"

Look at the child's hand.

"I think I'll take a little bite."

Gently nibble on the child's hand, making exaggerated smacking noises with your lips. If the child appears afraid, you might pretend to take a nibble.

The Spider Game

See the little spider
Crawling by you?
Here it comes-"Hello, spider."
There it goes-"Goodbye, spider."
See the little spider
Crawling on your leg (arm, head, finger, foot, etc.)?
Here it comes-"Hello, spider."
There it goes-"Goodbye, spider."

Materials: This can be done with no materials or with a spider finger puppet. Place the finger puppet on your finger or pretend your fingers are a spider. The child must be at least 20 months old developmentally to understand the pretend spider. If the child is afraid of spiders, you can use a turtle or any other animal.

Verse One: To begin the game so the child is not scared of the spider or of the action, have the spider crawl next to the child. As the spider crawls, you say, "Here it comes - Hello, spider." Then remove the spider from the child's sight (behind your back) and say, "There it goes - Goodbye, spider."

Verse Two: Now you can begin to crawl the spider on the child's body. Repeat the same process as before.

Remember, if the child is scared, this is not fun. If the child begins to get scared in the middle of this game (or any game), it is your responsibility to stop the game and say, "That was scary for you. I want to keep you safe. I am going to put the spider away, and we will not play that game again." Then immediately play one of the child's favorite games.

This Little Finger

This little finger came to school in a car.

This other finger rode the bus.

This tall finger rode her (his) bicycle

And this one chose to walk.

This thumb lived so-o-o far away

It had to go up the hill and down.

Up the hill and down,

Up the hill and down,

Up the hill and around,

To get all the way inside the school.

Preparation and Instructions: This interaction is modeled after the game, This Little Piggy. For parents, the first line of the poem can be changed to say, "This little finger went to school in a car." It is a wonderful interaction to use with children as they begin public or private preschool and kindergarten. Have the child sit on your lap so you can put your arms around the child, and hold his or her hand (palm facing toward you and the child). This puts you and the child in position so the child's fingers can easily be manipulated.

"This little finger came to school in a car."

Using your thumb and fingers in opposition, start at the base of the child's little finger, rub the finger up to the end, and give the finger a little squeeze. The squeeze will occur at the same time you say "car."

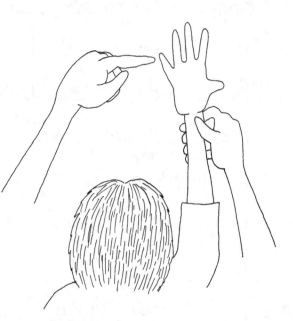

"This other finger rode the bus."

Repeat the activity with the ring finger, giving a little squeeze on the word "bus."

"This tall finger rode her (his) bicycle"

Continue with the massage of the tallest finger and then end with a squeeze as before.

"And this one chose to walk."

Repeat the process with the pointer finger.

"This thumb lived so-o-o far away"

As you say this line of the poem, wrap all your fingers around the child's thumb and give it a hug.

"It had to go up the hill and down."

With your pointer finger begin outlining the fingers. Start with the little finger and go up the side of the finger and down the other side. Do this in timing with the poem.

"Up the hill and down,"

Your finger is now in the valley between the little finger and the ring finger. Continue to trace the outline of the fingers, synchronizing the movements of up and down with the words.

113

"Up the hill and down,"

Continue tracing the fingers.

"Up the hill and around,"

At this point you are between the tall finger and the pointer finger. To finish this process, go up the pointer finger, over the top and down the side into the valley between the pointer finger and the thumb.

"To get all the way inside the school."

Tuck the child's thumb into his or her palm. Take each of the child's fingers and wrap them down over the thumb, one at a time, until all fingers are making a fist with the thumb on the inside. (This is to get the thumb inside the "school.") End the interaction by encircling your hands around the child's fist for a loving, gentle squeeze.

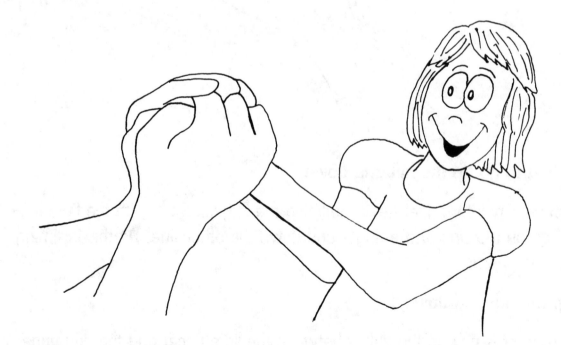

This Little Finger Goes Night-Night

This little finger on the end
goes cluck-cluck like a baby hen.

The next little finger on the hand

goes _____ like a big brass band.

(Make a noise in the space left blank)

This little finger goes tick-tock,

just like __child's name__ kitchen clock.

This little finger points to you
and says, I love you, yes I do.

The last little finger goes night-night.

I will kiss her (or him) and she will sleep tight.

Preparation and Instructions: Holding the child's hand, say the rhyme while touching the designated finger and making the appropriate noises. At the last line, after you kiss the little finger and say "she will sleep tight," take both of your hands and give the child's whole hand a big hug and squeeze.

Extension: With a surprised look on your face, you can add in a shocked voice, "What about the thumb? I forgot the thumb! I want to make sure every part of you sleeps tight. I must give it a kiss and tuck it in bed." After kissing the thumb, you can tuck it under the child's fingers as you assist the child in making a fist.

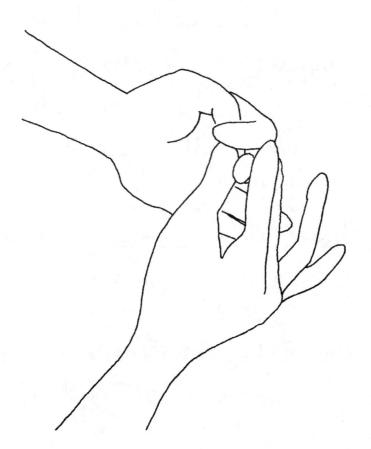

Today Is _____'s Birthday

Today is __(insert name of child)__ 's birthday.

Let's make her (him) a cake.

Mix and stir,

Stir and mix,

Then in the oven to bake.

Here is the cake so nice and round,

Frosted with pink and white.

We put five (any number) candles on the top

And blow out the birthday light.

Preparation and Instructions: This is a wonderful way to celebrate the birthday of a child. You will be picking the child up and laying him face up in your lap, so you want to be seated comfortably with your back supported. This is an especially nice way to wake children up on the morning of their birthday.

"Today is __(insert name of child)__ 's birthday."

With great love and joy say the first line, looking the child in the eyes.

"Let's make her (him) a cake."

With excitement say this line. Rub your hands down the sides of the child's body from shoulders, down the arms, and down the sides of the legs.

"Mix and stir,"

Pretend to be mixing and stirring the child by massaging the arms, the hands, and the legs.

"Stir and mix,"

Continue the massaging process with some gentle wiggling and jiggling of the child's entire body.

"Then in the oven to bake."

Pick the child up and lay him in your lap. Your lap is the pretend oven. It is fun to make a humming sound as if the child is cooking.

"Here is the cake so nice and round,"

Take the child out of the oven by removing the child from your lap and laying him out in front of you. Outline the child's head and cheeks with both of your hands.

"Frosted with pink and white."

Pretend to put frosting on both of the arms.

"We put five (any number) candles on the top"

Help the child hold up as many fingers as the child is old.

"And blow out the birthday light."

Have the child "blow out" his own fingers. As he does so, tuck the fingers away and snuggle the child into your arms. You can sing the traditional Happy Birthday song to the child while you rock him in your arms.

Two Blackbirds

1. Two little blackbirds
Sitting on a hill,
One named Jack and
The other named Jill.
Fly away, Jack.
Fly away, Jill.
Come back, Jack.
Come back, Jill.

2. Two little blackbirds
Watching a show,
One named Fast and
The other named S-l-o-w.
Fly away, Fast.
F-l-y a-w-a-y , S-l-o-w.
Come back, Fast.
C-o-m-e b-a-c-k, S-l-o-w.

3. Two little blackbirds
Looking at the sky,
One named Low and
The other named High.
Fly away, Low.
Fly away, High.
Come back, Low.
Come back, High.

4. Two little blackbirds
Sitting in a loft,
One named Hard and
The other named Soft.
Fly away, Hard.
Fly away, Soft.
Come back, Hard.
Come back, Soft.

Preparation and Instructions: Have the child sit on your lap with his back to your stomach, so you can reach around him with your arms and manipulate his hands. Hold the child's hands in your hands as if you were going to control a puppet. Have the child make a fist and point his thumb up in the air. Start each verse with both the child's hands behind his back.

"Two little blackbirds, sitting on a hill, One named Jack and"

Bring out one of the child's hands with the thumb pointing up.

"The other named Jill."

Bring out the other hand.

"Fly away, Jack."

Fly that hand back behind the child.

"Fly away, Jill."

Fly that hand behind the child's back.

"Come back, Jack. Come back, Jill."

When the birds are called back, fly them to the front position.

The Other Verses: The rhyme proceeds in the same format for all verses. The only variation is the way the birds fly. If the bird is named Fast, move the child's hand very rapidly and speak very rapidly. When the bird's name is Slow, move and speak slowly. The same holds true for Hard and Soft.

Extensions: You and the child can make up endless variations to the names of the birds. Have fun!

Warm Hands

Warm hands warm,
Do you know how
To warm your hands?
I'll blow your hands now!
Warm hands warm,
Do you know how
To warm your hands?
I'll rub your hands now!

Preparation and Instructions: This is a wonderful interaction in the winter or anytime you feel the child needs a "warming up."

"Warm hands warm"

Take the child's hands in yours and rub them rapidly to warm them up.

"Do you know how"

Begin to move your hands over the child's hands.

"To warm your hands?"

Cup your hands over the child's hands. Make sure you are at eye level with the child.

"I'll blow your hands now!"

Bring the child's hands, cupped within your hands, to your mouth and blow air gently into the cavity created. The warm air from your mouth will warm the child's hands.

Verse Two: This is done the same as in verse one; however, instead of blowing, this time you rub the child's hands with your hands.

You Have Ten Little Fingers

You have ten little fingers
And they all belong to you.
They are so very wonderful,
Look what they can do.
We can shut them up tight.
We can open them up wide.
We can put them all together
And we can see what's inside.
We can open them up
and trace all the lines.
We can put them together
Matching yours and mine.

Preparation and Instructions: Sit either with the child in your lap, with her back to your front, or sit facing each other. You will be manipulating both of the child's hands.

"You have ten little fingers and they all belong to you."

Touch each of the child's ten fingers as you say these two lines.

"They are so very wonderful, look what they can do."

Continue to touch the child's hands and admire them. Look at the child with a sense of pride.

"We can shut them up tight."

Take the child's hands and put them together into a tight ball.

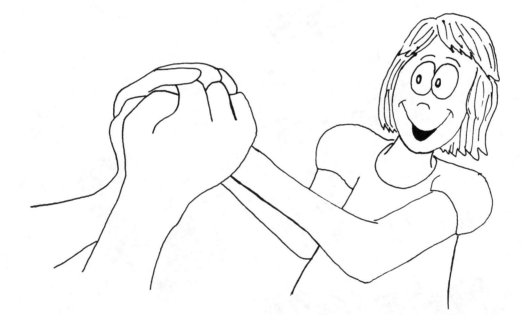

"We can open them up wide."

Open the child's hands and extend her fingers out wide, as the line indicates.

"We can put them all together and we can see what's inside"

Tuck the child's hands together with yours and open them slightly to look inside.

"We can open them up and trace all the lines."

Open the child's hands and use your finger to trace the lines in the child's hands.

"We can put them together matching yours and mine."

Hold your hands up and match them with the child's hands. Put your thumb and fingers up against her thumb and fingers.

Your Fingers Are So Sleepy

Your fingers are so sleepy,

It is time they went to bed.

First you, baby finger,

Tuck in your little head.

Ring finger, now it's your turn.

Then comes the tall one, this is just great!

Pointer finger, hurry, because it's getting late!

Is everyone here and nestled in?

No, there is one to come.

Move over, everyone, here comes the thumb!

Preparation and Instructions: This is another wonderful interaction for naptime or bedtime. Keep your voice calm and soothing.

"Your fingers are so sleepy"

Yawn and speak slowly and softly. Hold the child's hand in one of your hands, palm facing upwards.

"It is time they went to bed."

Take your other hand and cover one of the child's hands as to symbolically cover it up.

First you, baby finger,"

Remove your outer hand and begin to put the fingers to bed. Begin with the little finger and tuck it into the child's palm and hold it there.

"Tuck in your little head."

Give that finger a gentle rub.

"Ring finger, now it's your turn."

Tuck down the next finger with the same loving care.

"Then comes the tall one, this is just great!"

Continue as before.

"Pointer finger, hurry, because it's getting late!"

Increase your speed of speech when saying this line, remembering to keep your tone soft.

"Is everyone here and nestled in?"

Massage the tops of the fingers and the child's knuckles.

"No, there is one to come."

With a surprised and concerned face, discover the thumb.

"Move over, everyone, here comes the thumb!"

Bring the thumb in with the other fingers and wrap your hands snugly around the child's hand, sending the message of security and comfort.

You've Been Gone

You've been gone and
You've been missed.
Here's an angel
For a good morning kiss.

Preparation and Instructions: This is a great "welcome back" ritual. Maybe a teacher with a child who has been absent or a parent whose child has been on a sleepover at a friend's house would enjoy this game. Having a stuffed angel or angel doll to use for the kiss adds a delightful dimension; however, you can pretend to be the angel and give the kiss yourself.

"You've been gone and"

Holding the angel doll or figurine so the child can see it, say the first line of the poem.

"You've been missed."

Continue in a delightful way to move the angel closer to the child.

"Here's an angel"

Build the excitement with your facial expressions of delight and the movement of the angel .

"For a good morning kiss."

Kiss the child with the angel. If this is a troubled child and you are beginning to build a relationship, kiss the child on his or her hand. As the trust level increases in the relationship from the child's point of view, you can move closer and closer to the child's cheeks. If the child is your own, give a big kiss on the face.

CHAPTER 6

Silly Interactions

"Angels can fly because they
take themselves lightly."

— anonymous

Greetings

Preparation and Instructions: The goal of this game is to be delightful and silly. When the child arrives at school or home from school, begin by shaking the child's hand and saying, "It is wonderful to see you." Then begin to get silly by shaking other body parts. Give a handshake to the child's foot, commenting, "It is wonderful to meet you, Mr. or Mrs. Foot." Shake the child's elbow, knee, pinky finger, ear lobe, hair, thumbs, and nose. Any body part will work.

134

Jelly Bean Toes

Preparation and Instructions: This is a wonderful game to use to get shoes and socks off of children. Sit with the child comfortably in front of you or even in a chair.

Hold onto one of the child's feet and begin to feel around inside the shoe. As you come to the toes say, "I think there are jelly beans in here. I love jelly beans. Yum Yum!" Proceed to take off the child's shoes while continuing a dialogue about jelly beans and how you can't wait to see them, taste them, etc.

After you get the shoes off, continue the same process with the socks. You might say, "Now I know they are jelly beans. But wait, they are moving. Maybe they are jumping beans instead of jelly beans." Be sure to have exaggerated facial expressions.

Pull off the socks and with surprise and delight say , "Well, they are toes, wonderful, beautiful, perfect toes!" Since many children have sand or dirt in their shoes, brush and clean the feet. If they are dirty, use a washcloth or wet wipe to gently wash the feet. Remember, this nurturing time is healing and loving.

My Face Has a Gift for You

Preparation and Instructions: This game is similar to the traditional game called Pick a Hand. In this old favorite, one person puts both hands behind his back with a secret object in one hand. Both hands are then brought from behind to be displayed to the person in front. The partner picks a hand and locates the object. If the person picks the hand with the object, he or she gets to keep the surprise. In this version of the game, again put your hands behind your back. The difference is there is no object. Simply put your hands behind your back and bring them in front of you where the child is waiting.

Ask the child, "Pick a hand, any hand." When the child makes a selection, make a funny face with a noise. You may choose to laugh out loud, giggle, growl, frown, sigh, etc. Make a face briefly and then put your hands behind your back again. Bring them forward and have the child select again. Make another face and continue the game. Keep the pace of this game fairly rapid.

Extensions: As the child becomes familiar with the game, allow the child to be the leader. As the child makes faces, you attempt to copy the faces made by the child.

136

Pick a Face

Materials: Cut pictures (or have the child cut pictures) of children's faces from magazines or children's books. Pick faces that have many different expressions on them. Paste the pictures on index cards and laminate them. You will also need a hand-held mirror.

Preparation and Instructions: Sit down with the child in your lap. Place the picture-face deck of cards on the floor face down and the mirror near. Have the child select a card from the pile. Look at the picture together. First, the adult copies the face on the card. The child is then asked to copy the face of the adult. As the two of you begin to make the faces, look at yourselves in the mirror. Make sure that both faces show up in the mirror.

Remember, the goal is not to be correct or make the "right" faces. The goal is to connect with the child, notice each other, love each other, and have fun.

Silly Interactions

Preparation and Instructions: These are delightful interactions with a child that alter the normal sequence of events or offer the element of surprise. The following are but a brief list of possibilities. The type of silly interaction you create is only limited by your imagination. Be playful and see how many different silly interactions games you can create in the classroom or home.

1. Put the child's shoes on the wrong foot.

2. Put the child's shoe (or sock) on the child's hand, then try the elbow.

3. Push the child's nose (belly button, etc.) and make a silly noise.

4. Comb the child's knee as if this were the natural and correct way to comb hair.

5. Blow raspberries (blow on the child's hand, stomach, etc., until it makes a noise).

Name the noises by saying, "There is an elephant in your hand. See! Right there!" Then blow another raspberry. Blow three "elephant calls" and ask the child, "How many elephants did you hear?" Sometimes the blows sound more like ducks. Use your imagination!

Yes and No

Preparation and Instructions: Tell the child, "When I say 'yes,' you are to say 'no.' You will copy how I speak exactly. If I say 'yes' very loud, you will say 'no' very loud." Begin by saying "yes" in your normal voice. Wait for the child to say "no" in her normal voice. If the child appears not to understand the game, model both the "yes" and the "no" for the child. Next say "yes" in a high squeaky voice; the child will respond "no" in a high squeaky voice. Change your voice, tone, and pitch as you continue the game. Make sure to exaggerate your facial expressions and sounds. You could also shake your head "yes," and the child in response would shake his or her head "no." You can get just as silly as you want. You can say "yes" while you laugh, sneeze, hiccup, or cry.

Remember: This is a wonderful game to play with a child who is a bit grumpy or wanting possibly to control another game you have attempted to play.

You Have a Present

Preparation and Instructions: This could be done at Christmas time, during Hanukkah, as part of a birthday celebration, or on return from a trip when the child asks, "Did you bring me anything?" After giving the child your gift, say "Do you have a present for me?" Then say, "I think I see one right there," and point to the child's hand.

Take some newspaper or any scrap paper and wrap the paper around the child's hand. Use this time to truly touch the child. Remember, the goal is not to wrap the hand but to connect with and touch the child. After the hand is wrapped, put a ribbon or bow on the top. Announce, "What a wonderful present. It just looks beautiful. I wonder what it is?"

Begin to unwrap the hand slowly, expressing all your feelings and thoughts out loud. You might say, "I am so excited. This is the best present ever. I just can't wait to see it. I know it will be just perfect."

As you get the hand partly unwrapped, reach under the paper to feel what might be inside. Comment on what you find. You might say, "Oh, what could this be? I think I found a finger. It is a wonderful finger, perfect length, and perfect color. Let me see. It is absolutely breathtaking in beauty. I wonder if there are more."

Continue this process until the hand is uncovered. With the hand out, begin then to examine the beauty of the present. You might say, "It is a lovely hand, with five fingers, three freckles, and these gorgeous veins." (Trace with your fingers.) Remember to touch the hand as you verbalize what you see. You may continue with the fingernails, knuckles, etc.

The greatest gift of all.

CHAPTER 7

Relaxing Games

"Success is the ability to fulfill your
desires with effortless ease."

— Deepak Chopra

Whoops Johnny!

Preparation and Instructions: Take the child's wrist and hold it up so that her fingers are pointing to the sky. Start at the base of the child's palm on the pinky finger side. Firmly and slowly trace your pointer finger along the outside edge of the palm and up the outside of the pinky finger. While you are tracing your finger, you will be saying "Whoops Johnny, Johnny, Johnny." Say as many Johnnys as needed until you reach the top of the pinky finger. On the downhill turn say, "Whoops!" as you slide firmly into the valley between the fingers. From the base of the pinky and ring finger, begin the climb up the outside of the next finger, proceeding in the same manner. The climb begins with "Johnny, Johnny, Johnny!" until again you again reach the top and begin the turn down into the next valley. At that point, in a slightly faster movement with more pressure, say, "Whoops!"

Ending Variations: Once you arrive at the thumb, you can end the rhyme in many different ways. Remember always to experiment with your own creations. One way is to "Whoops" right off the thumb like a skier and land somewhere else on the child, such as a knee or shoulder. Another ending is to climb to the top of the thumb saying, "Johnny, Johnny, Johnny," and this time instead of saying "Whoops," squeeze the thumb and say, "This is not a Johnny thumb, this is a _____ (add child's name) thumb." Then repeat the activity using the child's name instead of Johnny.

144

Hot Dog Game

Materials: This game can be played with a real or pretend baby blanket or beach towel.

Preparation and Instructions: Instruct the child to lie on and perpendicular to one end of the towel or blanket. Ultimately, you will be rolling the child in the blanket like a hot dog bun. You want to make sure that his or her head and feet are out of the blanket. Begin the game by saying, "I am going to pretend this towel is a hot dog bun and you are a hot dog. Lie down here on the bun. Boy, am I hungry! I sure would love a hot dog. Well, look here. I see a hot dog right in front of me. I need to put on some ketchup." Pretend to squirt ketchup on the child and rub it all around (massage the child). "I need some mustard." Continue to pretend putting as many things on your hot dog as you like. Once the hot dog has everything you like on it, roll the child up in the towel like a bun. After the child is rolled up, you can put him or her in your lap or leave him or her on the floor. Pretend to gobble up the hot dog. Take your cues from the child. If you see any sign of anxiety or fear, stop the game. Be careful when you roll the child up that the child is comfortable and there are no hurts.

Extension: You can roll the child up in the blanket and then say, "Oh, I forget to put the pickles on." Then unroll the child to put on pickles. Roll the child again. This allows you to roll the child securely in the blanket and unroll him until he becomes more comfortable being wrapped tightly.

Painting a Picture

Preparation and Instructions: Begin the game by saying to the child, "I think it is time for a family (or school) picture. Sit right here in front of me. I am going to paint a picture of you. I want to make sure I get those brown eyes, black hair and white teeth just right." Use one hand as the imaginary paint palette to mix the paints, and use your other hand, (and/or fingers depending on the size of the brushstroke required), as the pretend paintbrush.

Outline the child's head and face, describing what you are doing: For example you might say, "First I am going to make an outline of your head. I am tracing around your neck, over your ears, outlining your hair, around the top of your head, around the other ear, and down this side of your neck. Now I am

going to outline your hair, so I can mix some paint and color the hair just your perfect color." Then, mix the paint in your palette, making sure it is just the right shade. Proceed to color the hair, lightly touching the child's hair as if you are brushing on the color.

Next, paint the child's whole face and neck, putting on the base color. Do this while slowly and firmly as to massage the child's face. Now you are ready to paint all the details. Paint the child's eyebrows, nose, eyelashes, chin, lips, etc. Describe to the child exactly what you see: "I see blue eyes, so I must mix just the right color. I see brown eyebrows that go right over each eye." Say these words as you "paint" (touch) the child.

When finished, tell the child, "I now have a new picture of you, and I will keep this picture in my heart forever."

Extension: Instead of painting the child's portrait, you may want to sculpt the child's face or head. In this case, you will make a bust of your child instead of a picture. This is similar to the painting process but more like a massage, as you work the pretend "clay" (the child's skin and face) into shape.

Putting Lotion on the Hurts Game

Materials: You will need a bottle of hand lotion, preferably with a pump spout for dispensing the lotion.

Preparation and Instructions: Search the child for "boo boos." These can be old scars or new scratches. The size or intensity of the sore is not relevant. Begin the game by saying, "I am going to put some lotion on all your hurts. I see one right here. I will be very careful to put it on all these hurts." Continue looking over the child's body for hurts. If the hurt is old, lotion can go directly on the scar. If the hurt is new, be careful to encircle the wound. Put some lotion on one finger and apply it very gently.

It is important that you repeat the message, "I will take care of you."

Sometimes children will help you find the sores. While you are putting lotion on one sore, the child is locating the next sore. In this situation the child is distracting him-or herself from the healing moment. If this happens say, "There are so many hurts you want me to notice them all. I will find them. I won't forget. See this one here. I am putting lotion all around it."

Sometimes children will tell you stories of how they were hurt. It is important to listen to the child.

Extensions: Another game is played with bandages. You begin the game with at least two. Ask the child, "Where do these go?" The child will direct you to the spot to place the bandage. If it is a hurt, speak to the hurt, "I am glad I found you. This bandage is for you."

Tell Me When I Am at the End

Preparation and Instructions: This is a wonderful game to play by itself or in conjunction with either the Slippery Hands game, or the Putting Lotion on the Hurts activity. You can play the game with or without lotion. I recommend you start playing the game first with lotion. Sit with the child facing you. Begin the game by putting lotion on your hands first and then on the child's hand and arm. Beginning up close to the elbow or shoulder, encircle the child's arm and begin pulling your hands down the arm. Say to the child, "Tell me when I get to the end of your fingers." Slowly move down the arm occasionally saying, "Am I at the end yet?" Slowly continue from the arm to the hand and down the fingers until you get to the end of the longest finger. You might have to cue the child several times by saying, "Am I at the end yet?" If the child misses the end, simply state, "There it is - the end of your fingers."

Extensions: Repeat the process with the other arm. You can play this game with the legs and feet. You can also use baby powder.

Washing Up: Washing the child after using the lotion or baby powder is very helpful. It gives you the opportunity to nurture the child, touching the child further. This develops even more the body awareness and your relationship with the child.

Making a Cookie

Preparation and Instructions: Tell the child, "I am going to make a cookie. I think I will make a _____ (child's name) cookie. First, I need to mix the ingredients."

Sitting comfortably on the floor, pick up the child and place him into your lap. Tell the child, "I am going to put you in the mixing bowl to get the cookie dough ready." With the child in your lap, begin to add some ingredients. You may pretend to dump in a cup or two of flour. You may want to add milk, sugar and salt. Then you can put in several eggs. To put in the eggs, gently tap the top of the child's head with your knuckles, then open your hand lightly touching the child's head. This will give the sensation of an egg being cracked and dripping down over his head. Ask the child if there are other ingredients he wants in the dough, and then add them. Then begin to mix the ingredients by shaking and circling the child in your arms, making whirring blender noises to accompany the actions.

Then take the child "out of the bowl" (off your lap) and lay him on the floor in front of you. Using your hands as a pretend rolling pin, flatten out the dough by patting and massaging the child's arms, legs, torso, hands, and feet. Do this slowly and firmly so as not to tickle. This will be similar to a gentle massage, as you knead and spread out the cookie dough.

Now it is time to cut out the cookie. Trace the outline of the child's body with your finger or the edge of one hand. Do this firmly so that the child is aware of your touch. You might say to the child, "I am cutting out the head, the arms, the fingers and the legs of this cookie."

Then tell the child, "It is time to bake the cookie." Pick the child up and put him back in your lap. This time your lap is the pretend oven. Gently rock the child back and forth as he continues to cook. You may want to set a pretend timer. After some cooking time, you could make a bell sound or say "Ding." Look down to see if the cookie is done. Check the arms, legs, and face to see if the child is done. You could say, "Let me see if this hand is done; is this arm done?" etc. Sometimes the child may say, "I am not done yet." This means that the child is enjoying being held and rocked, and would appreciate a little more cooking time.

Finally, take the child out of the oven (off your lap) and lay him on the floor again, in front of you. Say to him, "The _____ (child's name) cookie is done. Now it is time to taste it. I am going to taste this finger (give it a kiss or a pretend nibble). Now I am going to taste this toe." Continue with different body parts until the cookie has been eaten. The child will guide you to what is comfortable for him.

Notice when the child offers parts of his body to be nibbled on. If a child holds up his foot, say, "Your foot is saying I want to be eaten." If he holds up his hand, you might say, "Your hand wants me to taste it." Describing what the child does encourages continued interaction with you.

Rub and Dry

Materials: You need a spray bottle with water in it and a terry cloth towel.

Preparation and Instructions: Have the child sit on your lap. Tell the child you are going to play Rub and Dry. Using a spray bottle, spray water on the child's hand. Remember, always tell the child what you are going to do before you do it. After the hand is sprayed, take the terry cloth towel and dry the child's hand, using this time to massage the child's hand and fingers. You might say, "I am drying off ____child's name____'s perfect hand. This perfect hand has five fingers, little hairs on it, five freckles, and two scars." Continue with the other hand. It is more predictable (and therefore more relaxing) to spray one hand, then the other. You can also do the child's arms and feet.

Extensions: Have the child move the body part that was sprayed and you catch it with the towel. He or she could hide the arm and you could find the magic button. That brings the arm back to be sprayed. You could also have the child put a hand on a piece of colored construction paper. As you spray the child's hand, the paper will get wet. When the hand is removed from the paper, the dry areas will create a hand print.

Hand Lotion Games

Materials: You will need a bottle of hand lotion, wet wipes, and/or a washcloth.

Preparation and Instructions: Take an abundant supply of hand lotion, and put it all over your hands. Then, take the child's hands and rub the lotion on her hands, rubbing it all over in a mutual massage fashion. While rubbing the lotion, you might say to the child, "I am going to put lotion all over this hand, this finger, this thumb, this wrist, and even up on this forearm." Once the lotion is applied, any one of the following games can be played.

Your Hands Are Getting Away!

In this game tell the child, "I am going to hold on to your slippery hands and not let them slip away." As you do this, begin to lean backwards and allow your hands to slip off the child's hands or forearm. Hold tightly as this occurs, so that the child feels a good massage motion as the arms and hands begin to slip apart. As the hands are slipping say, "Oh no! Your hands are getting away. I will hold on to them tight. They are slipping, they are slipping." Eventually the arms and hands separate. Repeat the game saying, "They got away from me that time, but it won't happen again!"

Who's on Top!

Take the lotion-covered hands and alternate stacking hands. First, put your hand palm down on the bottom of the pile. Put one of the child's hand's next, then your hand on top of that hand, and finally the child's other hand rests on top of the pile. Say, "Look, your hand is on top. Mine is on the bottom." As you say this, wriggle your bottom hand so that the child feels it move. Then move your hand from the bottom to the top. Then say, "Look, my hand is on top, and your hand is on the bottom." If the child does not wriggle her hand, encourage her by saying, "Are you down there? I can't feel you." Continue the game, increasing the speed at which you change the stacked position.

Extensions: Similar type games can be played with the child's feet. Lotion your hands and the child's feet and play "Your Feet Are Getting Away!"

CHAPTER 8

Hide and Seek Games

"You have come here to find what you already have."

— Buddhist Aphorism

Find the Stickers

Materials: Use commercially bought stickers.

Preparation and Instructions: Before you see the child, take four or five stickers and hide them on your head. At the beginning make sure they are easily found. You may want to put one sticker on each ear lobe like earrings, and one sticker on your forehead, under your hair if possible. Be creative!

Begin the game by saying to the child, "I have hidden four stickers on my face. You are to find them and take them off and give them to me." As the child begins to look for them, use the skill of tracking. Tracking is simply saying out loud what the child is doing. It is similar to the radio announcer for a ball game. You might be saying, "You are looking over by my ears. Ah hah! You found one. Now you are taking it off very gently and handing it to me."

As the child hands you the stickers, put one sticker on each finger of one hand as a holding place. From this holding place you are ready to play the game again or conduct a variation of the game.

Extensions: One game or variation is called Sticker Swap. Once you have the stickers off your face, you can begin to play the Sticker Swap game by saying, "I am going to take this sticker off my thumb and put it on my chin." You proceed to do this. Then tell the child, "Take the sticker off my chin and put it on your chin." From this point you begin a turn-taking game whereby you remove the sticker from the child's face and place it on your face. The child then removes the sticker from your face and puts it on his face. Each movement of the sticker is said out loud. You speak for yourself and for the child unless the child catches on and begins to speak for himself. The dialogue might sound like this: "I am going to take the sticker off your chin and put it

58

on my nose. Now you are taking it off my nose and putting it on your (wait for the child's selection)."

Extensions: You can also reverse the direction of this game. In doing so, you would remove the sticker from your own face and put it on the child's face. You could also extend the game by playing with two or three stickers.

Tracking is an essential skill in playing these games.

Find the Yarn

Materials: You will need about five or six strands of yarn. Each strand can vary in length from 30 inches to 6 feet. It is best to have different colors for each strand.

Preparation and Instructions: Before meeting the child, hide the yarn on your body. You may want to put yarn up your sleeve, with just a tiny piece hanging out. You can put yarn in your pockets or socks, again leaving a piece sticking out for the child to spot. You can also put a yarn bow in your hair.

Begin the game by telling the child, "I have hidden four strands of yarn on my body. Find them and pull them out." As the child spots the tiny ends, he or she will begin to pull. Some of the strands will be short and some, humorously, will seem to go on forever. Track what the child is doing as in the game of Find the Stickers. You might say, "You are looking around my arms. You see the pink yarn. You are pulling and pulling and pulling."

Once the yarn is out, you can be creative in what to do with it next. You can measure the length of the child's body parts. You can stuff the yarn into the child's hand and have him throw it on a signal: "Ready, set, throw the yarn. Now find another piece of yarn." If the child has trouble locating the yarn, you can give helpful hints like, "I will give you a hint, it is below my knees," or "My eyes will look at it. Watch my eyes. My eyes are giving you a clue." Sometimes the child will need assistance. The goal of these challenging games is always success for the child.

Tracking is an essential skill in playing these games. Remember to keep tracking what you and the child are doing

Hello, Toes/Goodbye, Toes

Preparation and Instructions: Take off the child's shoes and socks. Once the shoes and socks are off, bring the child's foot close to your face or move your face close to the foot and say, "Hello, Toes." At this point you could look at them, blow on them, count them, touch them, or nibble at them. Quickly say, "Goodbye, Toes." As you say this, hide the toes from your sight. Then begin with a hide-and-seek dialogue: "Where did those toes go? I just had them in my hand. They were so lovely. Now I have lost them. Oh dear, what will I do? Maybe I put them here." (Search for the feet all over the child.) Once you find them, say "Hello, Toes." This begins the game over again.

Extensions: You can play the game with any body part. You can play with hands, knees, ears, etc.

Hide and Seek

Materials: There are as many Hide and Seek games as you can make up. Some of them may require props. In the suggestions below, you will need a food source (M & Ms, cookies, etc.) and cotton balls.

Preparation and Instructions: Hide and Seek games are really an extension of Peek-a-boo games. The list of games below is a beginning list. You will build upon this as new games emerge between you and the children you play with.

Hide the Cotton Ball: Have the child sit or lie down in front of you. Have the child cover or close his eyes (children usually like to peek and that is okay). Hide three or four cotton balls somewhere around the child's body. You may put them under the sleeve of the child's shirt, in a pocket, or stuck in a sock. Then tell the child it is okay to look and begin to search for the cotton balls. Of course you know where they are - you hid them. That is not the point. The point is the search. Begin by saying, "Where could that cotton ball be? Maybe it is behind the ears. No. I know, maybe in the mouth. Okay, you are tricking me. Is it in those ears?" Continue looking, touching, and talking, the sillier the better. You might say, "I need a hint." Ask the child to look with his eyes at where the cotton ball is, and you will follow his eyes to where he is looking.

Hide the Food: When you find the food, feed it to the child. It is important that you give the food directly to children. Food represents love; never tease children with food. You want the message to be, "I will take care of you. I see you. You are loved and lovable."

Extension: For older children, you may have them hide the cotton balls or food on themselves for you to find.

I'm Hiding

I'm hiding, I'm hiding.

No one will find me here.

I'll be as quiet as I can be

When anyone gets near.

And when they've looked all over,

Around and all about,

I'll jump out from my hiding place

And give a great big shout.

Materials: You will need two small baby blankets or beach towels.

Preparation and Instructions: Sitting side by side, you are going to cover the child and cover yourself. When you cover yourself, make sure you can see the child. In other words, do not cover your face entirely. Under your blankets say the rhyme above.

When you get to the part about a great big shout, both of you pop out from under the blankets. Your shout can be a number of things. The child might shout, "Here I am." In response you would say, "There you are and I am so glad. I thought you were gone. I missed you." The child might say, "Boo!" Your response might be, "You wanted to scare me. I see your brown eyes and black hair. I am glad to see you." Whatever the child shouts, your response is to send the message, "I see you. I am glad you are you. I missed you while you were gone."

Peek-a-boo

Materials: This can be played without any materials or with towels, scarfs, or any objects you or the child can hide behind.

Preparation and Instructions: This is a traditional game that most people have played. You may play the game by covering your face or the child's face. Begin the game by you or the child hiding behind one of the objects. Then proceed by saying, "Where is Ashley? Where could she be? She was just here. Is she in my shoe? Is she over here?" Continue until you find the child.

Extension: Sometimes children will initiate this game when you have originally planned to play another game. The child, instead of cooperating with you, hides her face. Some children will hide to avoid playing the game you started, in order to be in charge of the interaction instead of being in relationship with you. When this happens, understand that the child is saying nonverbally, "You can't see me. Do you care to look for me? Am I important enough to find? Or will you give up and leave me alone?" This also allows the child to have some control over when to be found. When the child changes the game to hide and seek, your response is important. Here are a couple of examples of what you could do:

1. You might say, "Where did Ashley go? I can't find her. Is she under the rug? Is she here in my shoe?"

2. If this does not draw Ashley out, you might continue with the following: "Who is behind those hands? I see one, two, three, four fingers and a thumb. I see fingernails, knuckles, etc. Over here I see an ear - that looks like Ashley's."

3. If you are still not successful, continue with the following: "Someone is hiding behind those hands. I am going to see if there is a magic button that will open those hands so I can find out who it is. Is this the magic button? No. Is this?"

Extensions: You can play Peek-a-boo with any body parts. You can throw a scarf over the child's hands, feet, etc. If the child is sitting on his hands, you can begin the game this way: "Timothy has no hands. Where could those hands be? Maybe they are in his ears."

Where Are Those Hands?

Clap our hands, one-two-three.
Play a clapping game with me.
Whoops, your hands have gone away.
I'll find your hands so we can play.

Materials: A small towel or scarf is needed for this activity.

Preparation and Instructions: Sit with the child facing you. Begin the game with a clapping pattern. If the child is very young or developmentally delayed, you can simply pat your hands together. If the child is capable, you can do a pattern. The traditional pattern is to pat your own thighs, clap your own hands together, and then clap the hands of the other person. Utilize the clapping pattern that creates the most success for you and the child. You will do this clapping pattern for the first two lines of the poem.

The second two lines of the rhyme offer a different experience. Take the towel and throw it over the child's hands to make them "disappear." Seek to find them in a silly manner. Look under the feet, under the armpits, and behind the ears. If he or she brings the hands out from under the towel, you might say, "Well, there they are. I was looking for them."

"Clap our hands, one-two-three."

Do the clapping pattern with the child as described above.

"Play a clapping game with me."

Continue the clapping in rhythm with the spoken words.

"Whoops, your hands have gone away."

Toss the towel over the child's hands.

"I'll find your hands so we can play."

In a silly way search for the missing hands.

Once the hands are found, start the rhyme again. Repeat as long as you are having fun. Remember to vary where you look for the hands and the way you find them.

Where Did It Go?

Preparation and Instructions: This is a familiar game to many adults. Many of us have played this game with our parents or grandparents. I remember my grandfather would come up to me and say, "I got your nose." Then he would show me his thumb between his fingers. I loved this game. The adult pretends to take the child's nose, finger, or other body part, but once you "take" a body part, it is important to put it back. You can use your imagination to help decide how to get the body part back on the child. Some suggestions of how to put back "taken" body parts are as follows:

1. Kiss it back on.

2. Blow it back on.

3. Pretend to nail it back on.

4. Take lotion and pretend to glue it back on.

Extensions: Sometimes the child will imitate this game and initiate the interaction by taking the body parts of the adult. The meaning of this is basically "I like you enough to want to have a part of you." The child in this experience is saying, "Do you like me enough to play my game? Will you come looking for me without your eyes? Can you breathe without your nose? Can you find me without your hands? Will you trust me to give it back to you?" Your response to the child taking a part of you is important. As the child begins this game, you might respond, "What happened to my eyes? I can't see Karen. Where did she go? This feels like her fingers, feels like her toes," etc. Or if the child takes your mouth, you might mumble, "I can hardly talk. Is there a magic button I can push to get my mouth back so I can talk to Karen?"

Remember: always put back taken body parts.

CHAPTER 9

Cuddling and Snuggling Games

"The time to relax is when you
don't have time for it."

— Sidney J. Harris

Blanket Swing

Materials: This game requires two adults and a sturdy blanket large enough to hold the child.

Preparation and Instructions: Lay the blanket on the floor and position the child on it. Each adult holds two corners of the blanket. On a signal given by an adult, the child is lifted up. The adults swing the child in the blanket and sing a song. The child is placed back on the floor on a signal. Verbally track the landing so the child knows exactly what is about to happen. You might say, "Let's put her bottom down first, then her feet, and carefully lay her head down."

There are many lullaby tunes that can be sung as you swing the child gently from side to side. Songs such as "Rock-a-bye, Baby" or "Brahms' Lullaby" are very soothing. If you choose to sing "Rock-a-bye, Baby," I suggest you change the ending of the song. The traditional ending goes:

When the bough breaks,
the cradle will fall.
And down will come baby,
cradle and all.

To send a more secure message to the child, the following ending is recommended:

When the bough breaks,
the cradle will fall.
And I will catch the cradle,
baby and all.

Row, Row, Row Your Boat

Row, row, row your boat
Gently down the stream.
Merrily, merrily, merrily, merrily,
Life is but a dream.

Preparation and Instructions: Sit on the floor with your legs crossed. Point to the space created in your lap and say to the child, "Come and get in the boat." Have the child sit in your lap with the child's back to your front. Put your arms around the child, holding her snugly. Once the child is in position, you are ready to begin the journey.

Tell the child, "The sea is calm, the sun is shining on our faces, and all is well." Rock gently side to side and back and forth as you sing the song. Use this time to snuggle and cuddle and enjoy the calmness of being together. The child may or may not choose to sing with you.

After the first verse say to the child, "The winds are coming (make wind noises), the seas are rising (increase the rocking side to side), it looks like a storm!" At this point, rock the boat intensely, falling from side to side and over backwards if you are comfortable with that. Give the child a good ride while saying, "I am going to hold you tight and keep you safe." Increase your snuggling action with the child and get really close as you bump around in the rough seas.

After singing the song one time in stormy seas say, "The storm is over, the sea is calm, the sun is shining on our faces, and all is well." Return to the gentle rocking side to side and back and forth, singing the song once again.

Snuggle Up

Preparation and Instructions: Many classrooms and homes provide a "safe place" for children. This is an alternate to time out. A safe place is where children who are feeling rejected, alone, anxious, or angry can go to return to a more peaceful inner state. This cannot occur unless they are first taught how to "experience" the place. A bean bag is a wonderful safe place because it almost hugs you when you sit in it. If you are going to use a bean bag, sit in it, holding the child and a transition object such as a teddy bear. While sitting in the bean bag, hold the child and sing the following to the tune of "Rock-a-Bye Baby":

Snuggle up, children,
In your safe place.
You can go there,
To have your own space.
When you feel scared
And want to feel loved,
Just cuddle yourself
And the bear with a hug.

When you get to the last two lines of the song, hold the child and the bear tightly, giving an extra little hug. To teach the child what a safe place is and what it is for, this activity must be repeated over and over again. Eventually, the child will be able to go to the safe place alone and feel the same soothing feelings he or she felt with you.

Extensions: In any type of cuddling game it is helpful to have a hand fan around. If the child appears to be getting hot, you can use the hand fan to cool him off. You might say, "You look so hot. I am going to cool you off. I am going to see if I can make your hair move with this fan. There it goes. Can you feel your hair move?" You might want to have a mirror handy so the child can see the hair move. You can also fan hands, bottoms of feet, under the arms, and tummies.

Safe Place

CHAPTER 10

Touching Games

"Touch is the most intimate of our
senses and in reaching out to others,
the message is clear: I'm here, I'm close,
and I care. What a pity that many of us wait a
lifetime to discover this miraculous power."

— Leo Buscaglia

Castings

Materials: You will need a roll of aluminum foil.

Preparation and Instructions: This game involves the adult making a mold of some of the child's body parts with aluminum foil. To make a casting of the elbow, have the child bend his or her arm at a 90 degree angle. Place a small sheet of aluminum foil over the elbow. Shape the foil into a mold. Remove the castings and examine the mold with the child. This can be done with a number of body parts, including but not limited to the following:

1. ears

2. nose

3. fingers

4. foot

5. hand

6. head

Handshake

Preparation and Instructions: To begin the game, greet the child with a big smile, "Good morning," and a regular handshake. As you are holding the child's hand, tell the child, "We are going to play a handshake game. After I shake your hand, I am going to add on to the handshake with another movement." You may do the handshake, then pick up your thumbs and touch them together. Repeat the two-part handshake again: shake hands and touch thumbs. Then add another movement to your handshake; this may be sliding the hands apart. Repeat the handshake: shake hands, touch thumbs, and slide apart. By now the child will have an idea of the game. Ask the child to add the next movement to the handshake. It may be a High Five. Repeat the sequence: handshake, touch thumbs, slide apart, and a High Five.

Depending on the developmental age of the child, you can add as many movements as possible. Once the child becomes familiar with the game, you may take turns adding movements to the handshake. (If you are a teacher playing this game, see if the child can remember the handshake throughout the day and in days to come.)

Extensions: Instead of doing handshakes, play the game Pinky Hugs. The game begins with the adult interlocking his pinky finger with the pinky finger of the child, announcing, "This is a pinky hug." Add different "hugs" onto the pinky hug as you did in the handshake game above. You can have elbow hugs, thumb hugs, and knee hugs. After you add on, remember to repeat the whole series, beginning always with a pinky hug.

Hello/Goodbye

Preparation and Instructions: This game is very similar in purpose and design to What Did You Bring to School? When you greet (or say goodbye) to the child, begin the game by saying, "It is so good to see you. I have been waiting for you. I am going to say hello to your hands, to each of your fingers, to your eyebrows, to your knees, to your shoulders," etc. As you say "hello" or "goodbye" to these parts of the child, you gently touch them. Your tone and facial expression should be one of adoration for the total child.

With each touch you consciously give a child, you help the child become more aware of himself. The child who is touched is enabled to recognize himself as an "I" and to recognize the toucher as another person with whom he can relate. The child who feels touch has a choice to accept the toucher (often demonstrated by moving closer to the adult or saying,"Do it again") or reject the toucher (often shown by moving away from the adult). Either way, the child will relate to the adult.

I Got Your Thumb

Preparation and Instructions: Have the child make both hands into fists and put them together. Take one of your hands, and encircle both the child's hands, using your hand as a blanket to cover the balled-up hands of child. If the child's hands are too big, cover only one of them.

Begin the game by saying, "Where could that thumb be?" With a curious look on your face, begin to search for the hidden thumb. To search, take your other hand and reach around in the cavity. As you reach in say, "Oh, here it is. I know this is it, I have found that thumb." Then with a surprised look, pull out one of the child's fingers between the crevices you created with your other hand (the blanket). Then say, "Well, that's not a thumb!" Then stuff the finger back down under your hand and begin the search again. Repeat the activity, pulling out various fingers. Once you are ready to end, you can actually find the thumb. When the thumb is out, you might say, "There it is, what a treat! There is that thumb. I must say hello to it." Then take your thumb and touch the child's thumb and say, "Hello thumb. I am glad I found you."

I Want More

One potato, two potato, three potato, four.
Five potato, six potato, seven potato, more!

Preparation and Instructions: Stand facing the child. Extend one of your fists and have the child extend to you one of her fists. With your other fist, touch your own fist and say, "One potato." Next, touch the child's fist and say, "Two potato." Continue alternating touches, reciting the above rhyme, until you touch the last fist and say, "More."

The person whose fist was touched last gets to pick what she wants more of from the picture selections to the right, choosing to have more hugs, more kisses, more holding time, or a back rub. The person points to the picture and the other person delivers the appropriate gift of "more." The game is then repeated. The next time, start the game by touching the child's fist first. This will add turn-taking to the game, and the child will then have the opportunity to give to the adult also.

If the child is a hurting child, play the game so that the child is the receiver of the more, until you receive verbal or nonverbal signs from the child that she is ready to choose to give.

I want more...hugs

...holding time

...back rubs

...kisses

Move What I Touch

Materials: This game can be played without any materials, or it can be played with many types of textured objects, which you will use to touch the child. Items such as feathers, terry cloth washcloth, silk scarf, and even sandpaper are fun.

Preparation and Instructions: Have the child lie down on the floor in front of you. Tell the child, "I am going to touch a part of your body with my hand (finger). I want you to move just that part of your body. The first body part I am going to touch is your pointer finger. See if you can move that finger and nothing else. Well, you did it. You just moved that one finger. You are good at this game. I am going to make it harder now. I am going to touch your whole hand. Well, look at that. You can do that too. The rest of your body was perfectly still. You kept your legs still (rub your hands over the child's legs). You kept your face still (rub your hands over the child's face)." Continue with the game in the same spirit as indicated above.

Extensions: Have the child close his or her eyes and play the game. Touch the child with different textured objects. Remember, do not tickle. This is a wonderful game for children with developmental delays or with extreme distractable or impulsive behaviors. It helps the child integrate and then differentiate body parts. Many children coping with hyperactivity have trouble moving just one part of their body. When one part moves, the whole body moves.

My Hand Is Stuck

Preparation and Instructions: This game begins by placing your hand on the child and saying, "My hand is stuck." Pretend it is indeed stuck and you can not remove it no matter how hard you try. Next, look for the "magic button" so that your hand becomes free. To do this you might say and do the following:

"I wonder if the magic button is here?"

Squeeze the child's thumb.

"No, it is not there."

Continue to struggle with your hand stuck on the child.

"Maybe it is here."

Push on the child's knee.

"Nope! Now where can that button be?"

Look all around the child.

"I see it. I know where it is!"

Take one finger and push on the child's forehead, simultaneously freeing your own hand from the shoulder.

Extensions: You can play this with any body part. My foot is stuck, my thumb is stuck, etc. Remember that when you play this game with children who are hurting, stay away from their stomach and face.

You Touch My Nose

Materials: You will need to know the Ella Jenkins' song entitled, "You'll Sing a Song and I'll Sing a Song." Ordering information regarding this children's tape is in the reference section of this book. The original words to the song go as follows:

You'll sing a song

And I'll sing a song.

We'll all sing a song together.

You'll sing a song

And I'll sing a song

In warm and wintry weather.

Preparation and Instructions: Sitting face to face with the child, singing to the tune of the above Ella Jenkins' song, begin the interaction by singing the revised song as indicated on the next page:

I'll touch your knee,

You'll touch my knee.

We'll touch our knees together.

I'll touch your elbow,

You'll touch my elbow.

We'll touch our elbows together.

I'll touch your (forehead, ears, toes, etc.),

You'll touch my (forehead, ears, toes, nose, etc.),

We'll touch our _____ together.

As you sing the song, do the actions indicated by the words. You can add any body parts or any actions (swing my arm, pull on this finger, wiggle your fingers to the tune). A fun way to end the interaction is:

I'll wave goodbye,

You'll wave goodbye.

We'll wave goodbye together.

192

What Did You Bring to School Today?

Preparation and Instructions: Say to the child, "What did you bring to school today?" Then begin taking inventory of all the body parts the child brought to school. You might say, "Oh, I see you brought your thumb, your shoulders, your two ear lobes," etc. As you state the body parts, touch each and every one. It is important that you do NOT mention any articles of clothing or other objects. The focus is on touching the child and having the child experience you and himself through the interaction. Focusing on material items sends the message that what we own or possess is more important than who we are. Children who do not have many possessions soon learn to feel that they are in some way inadequate.

Extensions: To continue with noticing the child, you can count the number of freckles on one arm. You can measure the length of a finger and see if it is the same as the length of the nose. You can do this measuring with string or a fruit stick that is sold at grocery stores. If you use the fruit stick, the child can eat it after the experience.

CHAPTER II

Physical Contact Games

"If play is to be genuine, it must be lighthearted and pursued without purpose. That is why we usually fail if we try to have fun."

— Larry Dossey

Blanket Volleyball

Materials: You will need a towel, baby-size blanket, and a balloon or some type of nerf ball.

Preparation and Instructions: The adult holds two ends of the blanket, and the child holds the other two ends of the blanket. On the signal given by the adult, a ball is placed in the middle. The goal is to toss the ball in the air and catch the ball in the blanket.

Remember: It is important that before you play this type of game with a young child, the relationship must be based on trust, fun, and reciprocity. The child must cooperate with you for this to be fun. If the child is wanting control as opposed to being in relationship, the game will deteriorate into a power struggle. To structure this game:

1. Be sure the child is emotionally capable of cooperating with you.

2. Clearly state the goal of the game: "Our goal is to work together and toss the ball and catch it. We can count how many times we are able to do this."

3. Clearly give a signal: "The signal to begin the game will be ready, set, go."

4. Do not put the ball on the blanket until just before you give the signal.

Body Drawing Games

Materials: Gather paper as large as the child, black construction paper, magic markers, baby powder, and hand lotion.

Preparation and Instructions: Tracing the child's body on a piece of paper or tracing individual body parts provides the child the opportunity to see and experience his body. There are a number of ways to conduct these interactions. Below are just a few examples:

1. Have the child lie on a piece of paper larger than himself. Take your marker and trace the outline of the entire child. It is helpful to track what you are doing as you are doing it. For example, you might say, "I am going around your arm and around your little finger, the next finger," etc.

2. Trace the child's hands or feet on a piece of construction paper. Describe what you are doing as suggested above.

3. Place a large amount of lotion on the child's hand and fingers, palm side up. Literally cake it on, without rubbing it in. Place the child's hand on black construction paper to make a print, then lift the child's hand straight up from the paper, leaving a lotion hand print. Take baby powder, sprinkle it on the paper, and move it around. Have the child help you blow off the excess powder. This is best done on a signal you provide. To structure this you might say, "When I give a signal we are going to blow the powder off the paper. The signal will be 'blow.' I will say 'One, two, three, blow,' and we will blow. Get ready. 'one, two, three, blow.'" To help the child wait for the signal and be successful, remove the construction paper from view while you are giving the child directions. Once the powder is removed, a very distinct hand print will be left on the paper. The print will even show the lines in the child's hands. Look at the hand print with the child and compare the print with the child's real hand and lines.

Cotton Ball Blow

Materials: You will need cotton balls and either a table top or stack of pillows.

Preparation and Instructions: Position yourself across from the child with a playing surface in between you. You could both lie on your stomachs on the floor facing each other. Sometimes it is more comfortable to sit at a table across from each other. Hold the child's arms with your arms to outline the playing field, then place a cotton ball in the middle of the field. On your signal both of you will begin to blow. The object of the game is for the child to blow the cotton ball over to your chest, and then, you blow the cotton ball over to the child's chest (or off the table, as the case may be).

Important Points to Remember: This is **not** a competition. The child may attempt to turn it into one. To structure the game to reduce or prevent this, you might want to do the following:

1. Begin the game by saying, "This game is called Cotton Ball Blow. I will give a signal, and we both will blow the cotton ball to see where it goes. You will try to blow it over to me, and I will try to blow it over to you."

2. Tell the child the signal. "the signal will be ready, set, go. When I say go, you and I will begin to blow."

3. Do not remove your hand from the cotton ball until you say go. This allows the child to begin on your signal and be successful.

4. If the child comments, "I won! I won!" you can simply respond by saying, "You blew the cotton ball over to my side.

5. Verbally track the results of each blowing encounter. "YOU blew the cotton ball, and it hit our arms and flipped off the table."

Guess What I Am Writing (Drawing)?

Preparation and Instructions: To start this game have the child turn around, so his or her back is available to you as "pretend paper" Tell the child, "I am going to write (or draw, depending on the level of the child) something on your back. See if you can guess what I am writing (drawing)."

Make sure that what you write or draw is easy enough for the child. The goal of the game is to touch the child and enjoy one another. It is not to test the child on his spelling or put him in a position where he might be unsuccessful. You may want to write letters or numbers. In this case tell the child: "I am going to write a letter on your back. See if you can guess what letter it is." For younger children, you may want to draw a simple shape such as a square or circle.

Extensions: You can use any part of the child to write upon, from the back of a hand to the bottom of the feet. (Remember, tickling is aggression for some children.)

You can also play a game called Two on a Pencil. In this game you will need a piece of paper and a marker of some sort (crayon, magic marker, pencil, or pen). Both of you hold the same pen; however, you guide the child's hand to write the child a note. You might write, "I am glad to see you," or other statements that celebrate the relationship between the two of you.

200

The Big Crash

Preparation and Instructions: Pick the child up in your arms and swing her around. Stop swinging and suggest to the child that she become an airplane or a bird. Hold her as she flies and then pretend that the airplane had a crash or that the bird got caught in a storm and flew into a tree. This gives you the opportunity to look over the child to see what needs loving and healing and find fun ways to attend to the parts before taking off again. You might say, "Oh no, the airplane has had a big crash. I will check to see if anyone got hurt. This arm looks good, these eyebrows are okay," etc.

This game involves fantasy. Fantasy is an important component of a relationship between you and the child. Fantasy ultimately allows the child to continue the relationship with you when you are not there. It also can enhance the development of the child's memory and thinking.

Fantasy can be used by some children as a means to escape from the intimacy of the moment and from being present. Intuitively, you will know when this is happening. If you think the child is using fantasy to escape from being engaged with you, shift the game from one that involves fantasy to one that requires the child to focus on his or her own body. A quick way to do this is to notice something about the child you have not seen before. You might say, "Look at this. I have not noticed this before. You have a freckle right here next to your elbow." This will bring the child back to the present moment with you.

The Cat and the Bunny

Creeping, creeping, creeping,
Comes the little cat.
But the bunny with the long ears
Hops like that.

Preparation and Instructions: This game involves more physical activity than many of the other interactions because you must be able to lift the child in order to play. Stand behind the child and prepare to move her body through these motions.

"Creeping, creeping, creeping"

From behind the child, place your arms under the child's arms (so the child's armpits are resting on your arms) and hold onto the wrists. Move the child's arms in a creeping movement.

"Comes the little cat."

Continue to move the arms in a creeping motion. You might want to add a "meow" at the end of the line.

"But the bunny with the long ears."

Take the child's hands up to the side of the head like big bunny ears.

"Hops like that."

Pick the child up by using your arms under her armpits and take her for a three-hop ride. The hops would coincide with the words of the poem.

Extensions: Change the movement at the end of the rhyme. You could say "swings like that" as you swirl the child around through the air. Try "leaps like that" "runs like that" "Skips like that" or whatever you come up with at the moment.

Walk and Stop

Preparation and Instructions: Pick the child up in your arms. Sing the following words with any tune that works for you: "You walk and walk and walk and . . . STOP!" As you sing this song, take steps with the child in your arms. When you say "stop," bring your body to a quick halt. Repeat the song as you move around the room carrying the child. (If the child has been sexually abused or you suspect this might have occurred, carry the child like a baby in your arms. Do not have the child straddle you with his or her legs on your hips.)

Extensions: Change the movements as you carry the child. Change from walking to jumping. "You jump and jump and jump and . . . STOP!" Try swaying, swinging, marching, skipping, hopping, wiggling, and leaping. Let your imagination go!

References

For those who want to learn more about touching, attachment, and facilitating children's growth through play, a list of references is provided. I highly recommend each one of these books and am thankful for what the authors have taught me. Some of the books are more difficult to obtain so I have included information to ease the process.

Brody, V. A. (1993). The Dialogue of Touch: Developmental Play Therapy
  To order this book, please write to:
  Viola A. Brody, Developmental Play Training Associates
  519 Plaza Seville Court, Treasure Island, FL 33706

Bowlby, J. (1969). Attachment and Loss: Volume 1, Attachment. New York, NY: Basic Books, Inc.

Bowlby, J. (1973). Attachment and Loss. Volume II, Separation. New York, NY: Basic Books, Inc.

Bowlby, J. (1988). A Secure Base. New York, NY: Basic Books, Inc.

Brazelton, B., & Barnard, K. (1990). Touch: The Foundation of Experience. Madison, CT: International Universities Press.

Davis, P. (1991). The Power of Touch. Carson, CA: Hay House, Inc.

Jenkins, Ella. You'll Sing a Song, I'll Sing a Song
  To order this recording, call:
  Classic School Products, 1-800-394-9661. Ask for product number FR45010

Magid, K., & McKelvey, C. (1981). High Risk: Children Without a Conscience. New York, NY: Bantam Books.

Montagu, A. (1986). Touching: The Human Significance of the Skin. 3rd ed. New York, NY: Harper and Row.

Other works by Dr. Becky Bailey

There's Gotta Be a Better Way: Discipline That Works ($21.95)

10 Principles of Positive Discipline ($16.95)

Transforming Aggression into Healthy Self-Esteem ($16.95)

Preventing Power Struggles ($16.95)

Conflict Resolution ($16.95)

To order, call 1-800-842-2846, or write to:
Loving Guidance, P.O. Box 622407, Oviedo, Florida 32762

Dr. Bailey is available for workshops and keynote addresses. Her dynamic presentation style lightens as well as enlightens audiences. Call 1-800-842-2846 to schedule her in your area. Dr. Bailey's expertise is in positive discipline, and her new program of **Conscious Discipline** transforms school classrooms into school families where children choose to be cooperative.

Epilogue

Your children are not your children.

They are the sons and daughters of
Life's Longing for itself.

They come through you but not from you.

You may give them your love but not your thoughts,

For they have their own thoughts...

You may strive to be like them, but
seek not to make them like you.

For life goes not backward nor tarries
with yesterday.

~ Kahlil Gibran